THE GUINNESS HITS CHALLENGE

QUIZ MASTERS

PAUL GAMBACCINI
TIM RICE JO RICE
AND MIKE READ

GRRR Editorial Associate : Steve Smith

GUINNESS BOOKS

ACKNOWLEDGEMENTS

The four authors would like to thank the following for their help and cooperation:
Judy Craymer, Melanie Georgie, Sheila Goldsmith, Eileen Heinink, Jan Rice, *New Musical Express*, *Melody Maker* and *Music Week*

Editor: Alex E Reid

Design and layout: David Roberts

First edition 1984

© GRRR Books Ltd and Guinness Superlatives Ltd 1984

Published in Great Britain by

Guinness Superlatives Ltd

2 Cecil Court, London Road, Enfield, Middlesex

British Library Cataloguing in Publication Data

The Guinness hits challenge.
 1. Music, Popular (Songs, etc.)—
 Miscellanea
 I. Gambaccini, Paul
 780'.42'076   ML3470
ISBN 0-85112-417-8

Guinness is a registered trade mark of Guinness Superlatives Ltd.

Typeset, printed and bound in Great Britain by
Hazell Watson & Viney Limited,
Member of the BPCC Group,
Aylesbury, Bucks

INTRODUCTION TO THE CHALLENGE

Why have the authors of *The Guinness Book of British Hit Singles* written this book? Can it be they are tired of compiling facts and want to do something, anything, different for a change? Could it be they are fed up with seeing quiz books that underestimate the knowledge of the reader and have decided to come up with tests that pose a real challenge?

Is this book a symptom of the GRRR team's sadistic desire to see regular readers squirm as they encounter almost impossible brain teasers after having breezed through a few easy questions? Could it be the result of a bizarre New Year's resolution they have made to speak to each other in 1984 only in the interrogative? Is it in the realm of possibility that they have compiled this collection of mind-stretchers just because they enjoy this kind of thing?

Is it possible that they are impatient with getting letters from pop fans asking obscure questions like 'Vera Lynn sang a song about loving somebody, what was it?', 'What was the tune with a long guitar solo performed on television recently?', 'Where can I buy the hits of Jimmy Roselli?'. Can it be that, after nearly 7 years of this inquisition, they have decided to get their own back?

You mean the only point of this book is to have some fun?

PAUL GAMBACCINI
MIKE READ
JO RICE
TIM RICE
Directors, Grrr Books Ltd

QUIZ 1	THE NAME GAME

The answers to all these questions are names.

 **A**

1. Buddy Holly's lady who got married
2. Happy with Who
3. Hey said Jimi Hendrix
4. Hey said the Beatles
5. Hey said Paul
6. Reggae with the Piglets
7. Jilted
8. Amazing Ms
9. Brother Of Hot Chocolate
10. Brother of the Free
11. Don Partridge's girl
12. Olivia Newton-John's boy
13. Michael Jackson's rat
14. Dr Hook rang her mother
15. Bryan Ferry met him in Tokyo
16. Kid Creole is not her Daddy
17. Christopher Cross sang his theme
18. Don and Phil were her clowns
19. Shaky's number one girl
20. The fastest milkman in the West

 **B**

1. The Shadows' first vocal hit
2. Del took off his hat to him
3. Slade said gudbuy to her
4. Alvin's sweet cheatin' girl
5. Ray Stevens' tiny queen of the blues
6. Marc Bolan's only hit lady
7. Juniper Eccles
8. She helped the Beach Boys
9. Who had her pictures
10. Quo's girl (live at the N E C)
11. Four Seasons' alcoholic lady
12. Alex Harvey stole her from Tom Jones
13. Please don't ask about Herman's lady

14 Polk Salad lady with a song of her own

15 Robin Luke and Tommy Roe's darlin'

16 Lee Marvin played him, either James Stewart or John Wayne shot him, and Gene Pitney sang about him

17 His death was remembered by Rod Stewart

18 She owned Bob Dylan's farm

19 Janis Joplin's last LP

20 Lou Johnson and Adam Faith sent her a message

 C

1 Who Jessi Colter isn't

2 Elton John's middle name

3 Buddy Holly rocked around with her

4 Heart's dreamboat

5 Eddie Fisher and the Faces sang about her

6 Eaten by the Buoys

7 The gambler shot by Stagger Lee

8 The Indian maid loved by Running Bear

9 Soeur Sourire's inspiration

10 Herman thought she had a lovely daughter

11 John Fred recognised her through the disguise

12 Billy Paul had an adulterous thing going with her

13 Herman claimed he was a king

14 Paul McCartney's black dog

15 Strange things happen when Dickey Lee meets her

16 The Jaynetts watched her go round the roses

17 R B Greaves dictated to her

18 Chicago sang of the man from Peoria

19 Marcie Blaine and Susan Maughan wanted to be his girl

20 Evil lady of Scottish descent, according to BS&T

QUIZ 2	WE ARE FAMILY

The following song titles all contain names of members of the family.
Give the artists who made these records hits (a few of the more difficult entries were hits in America). If you get them all right, you should form a partnership with Pete Frame as rock's leading genealogists.

 **A**

1 'Don't Cry Daddy'
2 'Mamma Mia'
3 'Mama'
4 'Son Of My Father'
5 'My Old Man's A Dustman'
6 'Mama Used To Say'
7 'Grandad'
8 'Mama Weer All Crazee Now'
9 'Papa's Got A Brand New Bag'
10 'Papa's Got A Brand New Pigbag'
11 'Papa Was A Rollin' Stone'
12 'There's No One Quite Like Grandma'
13 'Mother And Child Reunion'
14 'Daughter Of Darkness'
15 'Daddy's Home'
16 'Brother Louie'
17 'Mrs Brown You've Got A Lovely Daughter'
18 'Daddy Cool'
19 'Son Of A Preacher Man'
20 'Like Sister And Brother'

 **B**

1 'My Son, My Son'
2 'Mother'
3 'Oh, Mein Papa'
4 'The Son Of Hickory Holler's Tramp'
5 'I'll Always Love My Mama'
6 'Mama Never Told Me'
7 'Mama Told Me Not To Come'
8 'Cousin Norman'
9 'Grandma's Party'

10 'Mother Of Mine'
11 'My Brother Jake'
12 'My Perfect Cousin'
13 'Mama's Pearl'
14 'Ma He's Making Eyes At Me'
15 'Father And Son'
16 'Family Affair'
17 'Mother's Little Helper'
18 'Me And Baby Brother'
19 'My Boy'
20 'Sister Jane'

 C

1 'Yes My Darling Daughter'
2 'My Child'
3 'My Mum Is One In A Million'
4 'Mother Nature And Father Time'
5 'My Dad'
6 'Mama's Boy'
7 'Papa Loves Mama'
8 'Papa Loves Mambo'
9 'Mother-in-Law'
10 'Mama Can't Buy You Love'
11 'Cousin Of Mine'
12 'My Son John'
13 'The Six Wives Of Henry VIII'
14 'Daddy Could Swear, I Declare'
15 'Brother'
16 'My Mammy'
17 'Mama Didn't Lie'
18 'Ma Says Pa Says'
19 'Family Of Man'
20 'Mama Look At Bubu'

<table>
<tr><td>QUIZ 3</td><td># I'M JUST A SINGER IN A ROCK 'N' ROLL BAND</td></tr>
</table>

QUIZ 3

I'M JUST A SINGER IN A ROCK 'N' ROLL BAND

Vocalists from the following bands also found success in the singles chart as solo artists. Who are they?

 **A**

1 Haircut 100
2 Kajagoogoo
3 Rolling Stones
4 Roxy Music
5 Blondie
6 T. Rex
7 Genesis
8 Four Seasons
9 Abba
10 Cockney Rebel
11 Manfred Mann
12 Thin Lizzy
13 Herman's Hermits
14 Police
15 Commodores
16 Supremes
17 Who
18 Walker Brothers
19 Led Zeppelin
20 Beatles

 **B**

1 Q-Tips
2 Generation X
3 Rainbow (1979 Line up)
4 Bread
5 Mamas and Papas
6 Slik
7 Deep Purple
8 10 C.C.
9 Equals
10 Mud

11 Moody Blues
12 Liverpool Football Team 1977
13 Drifters
14 Mott The Hoople
15 Monkees
16 Traffic
17 Wizzard
18 Yes
19 Zombies
20 Linx

 C

1 Dovells
2 Vinegar Joe
3 Rainbows
4 Raspberries
5 Ikettes (Ike and Tina Turner's backing vocalists)
6 Be Bop Deluxe
7 Temptations (1971 line up)
8 Ultravox (Mark 1)
9 Rubettes
10 Love Sculpture
11 Brinsley Schwarz
12 Kinks
13 Addix
14 Manfred Mann's Earthband
15 Yardbirds
16 Stone Poneys
17 Stealer's Wheel
18 Them
19 UK Subs
20 Buffalo Springfield

QUIZ 4	I KNOW WHAT I LIKE IN YOUR WARDROBE

Score one point for each correct answer.

1 Who sang 'Pyjamarama'?
2 Who wore an old brown shoe?
3 Before the two British cuts, who fashioned the original white sport coat?
4 Which Tamla artist laid his hat many years before Paul Young?
5 Whose red shoes did the angels want to wear?
6 Which group started off their chart life wearing their favourite shirts?
7 Not many people bought this pullover. Whose was it?
8 Matchbox wore black slacks in 1979. Which American group originally wore them?
9 Who leapt up and down and waved their knickers in the air?
10 As Rod Stewart said 'an old one will never let you down'

QUIZ 5	TRACKS OF MY TEARS

Listed below are three tracks from well known, or on occasion slightly less well known albums. All you have to do is name the album and the artists involved.

1 'Whole Lotta Love', 'The Lemon Song', 'Ramble On'
2 'Crippled Inside', 'Oh My Love', 'How Do You Sleep'
3 'Babylon', 'Vincent', 'Winterwood'
4 'Bed's Too Big Without You', 'Walking On The Moon', 'On Any Other Day'
5 'As Long As I Have You', 'Crawfish', 'Steadfast Loyal And True'
6 'Brown Sugar', 'Bitch', 'Sister Morphine'
7 'Cecilia', 'Only Living Boy In New York', 'Song For The Asking'

8 'Angel', 'I'd Rather Go Blind', 'Twisting The Night Away'

9 'Candle In The Wind', 'All The Girls Love Alice', 'Saturday Night's Alright for Fighting'

10 'Love Me Do', 'Misery', 'Anna'

11 'Oh Boy', 'I'm Looking For Someone To Love', 'Maybe Baby'

12 'Second Hand News', 'Dreams', 'You Make Lovin' Fun'

13 'Head Over Heels', 'One Of Us', 'Slipping Through My Fingers'

14 'Mowhok', 'Stand And Deliver', 'Picasso Visita El Planeta de Los Simios'

15 'All My Loving', 'Till There Was You', 'Money'

 **B**

1 'Alone Again Or', 'The Daily Planet', 'Andmoreagain'

2 'Back Seat Of My Car', 'Too Many People', 'Smile Away'

3 'I'm Gonna Love Her For Both Of Us', 'Read 'Em And Weep', 'Nocturnal Pleasure'

4 'He'll Have To Go,' 'Pledging My Love', 'It's Easy For You'

5 'Everything's Alright', 'Heaven On Their Minds', 'Strange Thing Mystifying'

6 'The Millionaire Waltz', 'Somebody To Love', 'Te O Toriatte'

7 'You Make Me Feel Like Dancing', 'Reflections', 'How Much Love'

8 'Leaves That Are Green', 'Richard Cory', 'April Come She Will'

9 'It's Not Cricket', 'Slightly Drunk', 'Goodbye Girl'

10 'If I Laugh', 'Moonshadow', 'Peace Train'

11 'Cold As Christmas', 'Kiss The Bride', 'One More Arrow'

12 'The Sound Of The Crowd', 'Open Your Heart', 'Get Carter'

13 'Jennifer', 'I Could Give You (A Mirror)', 'The Walk'

14 'Human Nature', 'The Girl Is Mine', 'The Lady In My Life'

15 'Baby Doll', 'Forever The Same', 'Numbers'

 **C**

1 'You've Lost That Lovin' Feeling', 'If', 'Help Me Make It Through The Night'.

2 'Me And Bobby McGee', 'Cry Baby', 'Mercedes Benz'

3 '3/5 Of A Mile In Ten Seconds', 'Come Up The Years', 'Somebody To Love'

4 'Wah Wah', 'If Not For You', 'It's Johnny's Birthday'

5   'All Along The Watchtower', 'I Pity The Poor Immigrant', 'I'll Be Your Baby Tonight'
6   'In The Gallery', 'Wild West End', 'Lions'
7   'Who'll Stop The Rain', 'I Heard It Through The Grapevine', 'Long As I Can See The Light'
8   'Superstar', 'The Letter', 'Delta Lady'
9   'Cut Across Shorty', 'Don't Ever Let Me Go', 'Boll Weevil Song'
10 'The Man With The Child In His Eyes', 'Them Heavy People', 'Room For The Life'
11 'Vino, Dinero Y Amor', 'No Room To Rhumba In A Sports Car', 'The Bullfighter Was A Lady'
12 'Elected', 'I Love The Dead', 'Sick Things'
13 'Early In The Morning', 'Coconut', 'Jump Into The Fire'
14 'Sweet Dreams', 'Good Year For The Roses', 'Brown To Blue'
15 'Say You Don't Mind', 'Daddy's Home', 'Oh No Don't Let Go'

| QUIZ 6 | NUMBER OF THE BEAST |

This quiz concerns songs with numbers in the title. All you have to do to earn your one, two or three points, corresponding to the group the question is in, is to give the correct number. On this quiz guessing could well earn you a point or two, since the answer must be a number of some magnitude.

1   How many steps to Eddie Cochran's heaven?
2   How many hours did it take Gene Pitney to reach Tulsa?
3   How many miles were Daddies Cliff Richard and Shep from home?
4   What numerical progression was in a Tom Robinson Top Ten title?
5   The Four Seasons sang about December of what year?
6   How many little boys did Rolf Harris sing about?
7   How many men in Leo Sayer's 1974 band?
8   How many days in the title of Michael Jackson's 1981 number one?
9   Sam Cooke's girl was only what age?
10 What numbers were as easy for Len Barry as A-B-C?

11 UB40 had two numbers in the title of the same hit. What were they?

12 How many nations under Funkadelic's groove?

13 How many ways to leave Paul Simon's lover?

14 How many miles high were the Byrds flying?

15 How many pints of lager did Splodgenessabounds order?

16 What time did the Who's train leave?

17 How many seas of Rhye did Queen sing about?

18 How many tons in Tennessee Ernie Ford's number one?

19 How many coins in Frank Sinatra's fountain?

20 What position in an imaginary chart did Pete Wingfield reach?

21 On what street was Harpers Bizarre's bridge?

22 How many minutes did the Selecter require for heroism?

23 What number address on Sunset Strip gave a hit TV theme?

24 What age did Paul McCartney speculate being on 'Sergeant Pepper's Lonely Hearts Club Band'?

25 With what number revolution did John Lennon deal on 'The Beatles'?

26 What day of the week did Hazel O'Connor sing about?

27 How many nervous breakdowns did the Rolling Stones sing about?

28 How old was Chuck Berry's sweet little girl?

29 How many tears did ? and the Mysterians cry?

30 Sheena Easton and Dolly Parton liked what numerical sequence?

31 How many days in the Beatles' week?

32 What was Keith's favourite temperature?

33 How many fine days did the Chiffons enjoy?

34 What was Manfred Mann's numerical countdown?

35 How old was the Regents' 1979 sweetheart?

 **B**

1 How many carats in the Associates' love affair?

2 What was the number of Roger Miller's engine?

3 How many lovers did Mary Wells have?

4 What were the chances in Cliff Richard's 1960 top three smash?

5 On what finger of the left hand did Martha and the Vandellas and later the Pearls place their rings?

6　How many bad apples did the Osmonds eat?

7　How many years in a 1981 Boomtown Rats charter?

8　How many pounds of clay did Craig Douglas and Gene McDaniels sing about?

9　How many ways did Tab Hunter chart his 1957 top five hit?

10　What number symphony of Mozart became a pop hit for Waldo de Los Rios?

11　How many of a kind were there of the Detroit Spinners' love affair?

12　The Electric Light Orchestra started their string of hits with, appropriately, an overture. What number was it?

13　What was the number of Amii Stewart's Disco Heaven?

14　According to the Mamas and Papas, at what time did young girls come to the canyon?

15　How many teens did the Sweet sing about?

16　Peter Noone of Herman's Hermits claimed he was which King Henry?

17　How many stars in Billy Fury's sky?

18　How many reasons did Connie Stevens have for her 1960 hit?

19　How many miles of bad road did Duane Eddy travel?

20　How many minutes did the Stranglers require?

21　How many strong winds buffeted Neil Young?

22　How many bells did the Browns ring?

23　What number gave Suzi Quatro a crash hit?

24　How many miles out was Mike Oldfield's aircraft?

25　By Medicine Head's arithmetic, how much is one plus one?

26　What fraction did Meat Loaf consider not bad?

27　According to Bob Dylan, how many of us must know sooner or later?

28　If you need a little loving, what number do you ring to reach Wilson Pickett?

29　Between what ages did Pat Boone sing about in 1959?

30　In what type of aircraft did Saxon fly?

31　The Four Tops lived in a house with how many rooms of gloom?

32　How many inches in T. Rex's rock?

33　How many miles did Edwin Starr travel?

34　Chicago had a Top Ten hit in 1970 with three different numbers in the title. What was the record?

35 What number was Brenda Lee on the Fool Parade?

 **C**

1 Bill Haley drank how many cups of coffee?
2 On what floor did Paul Nicholas find heaven?
3 Stevie Nicks sang about being on the edge of what age?
4 How many women did William Bell try to love?
5 The Adverts bemoaned it was no time to be what age?
6 Desmond Dekker and the Aces had a hit number with what number?
7 How many days on the road did Dave Dudley have left?
8 According to Mary Wells, what is easy for how many is so hard for one?
9 What was the number of Sammy Hagar's space station?
10 How many dollars did George Jones and Gene Pitney have when they cut a country duet?
11 What were the dimensions of Ken Dodd's 1964 hit?
12 Stephanie Mills and Orange Juice both sang about the same number of hearts. How many?
13 Gisele McKenzie suffered how many lonely days in her 1953 Top Ten hit?
14 How many years did Rosanne Cash ache?
15 Johnny Cash had a country classic concerning a flood. The water was how many feet high and rising?
16 What time was something special for the Lovin' Spoonful?
17 What times did the trains arrive in Jimmie Rodgers' 1963 recording?
18 How many summer nights in the Danleers' doo-wop classic?
19 In what year did Paul Davis have a love affair?
20 In 1955 Boyd Bennett and Frankie Vaughan both made the top 20 with what numerical title?
21 How special, numerically, was Larry Graham's girl?
22 How many miles did Michael Holliday travel in 1956?
23 How many ways did James Ingram give Quincy Jones a hit?
24 How many little fingers did Frankie McBride have?
25 What number does Tommy Tutone call for a good time?
26 How many little words did the Applejacks use in 1964?
27 How many minutes did the Trammps require?
28 What was the Rimshots' numerical countdown?

29 In 1960 both Brian Hyland and the Avons sang about little heels. How many?

30 How many little girls sat in the back seat?

31 How many steps to love for Brian Poole and the Tremeloes?

32 The Presidents had a soul smash in 1970. There were six numbers in the title. What were they?

33 How many steps for Rahni Harris and F.L.O. in 1978?

34 How many dollars did the Stylistics sing about?

35 The Stargazers had more tiny fingers than Frankie McBride had little fingers. How many did they claim to have?

QUIZ 7	THE END OR THE BEGINNING

If you insert the correct word into the bracket it will complete the title of one hit song and start the title of another. Find the word in each case and name the groups or artists that had hits with the songs.

 A

1 Living On An (. . . . .) Of Lost Souls
2 It Takes Two To (. . . . .) In Mono
3 Something's (. . . . .) Words
4 Rockabilly (. . . . .) Rouser
5 American (. . . . .) Woman
6 Eye Of The (. . . . .) Feet
7 Grandma's (. . . . .) Fears Two
8 Do Anything You Wanna (. . . . .) I Do
9 Do You (. . . . .) Games
10 Silence Is (. . . . .) Years

 **B**

1 Love Is (. . . . .) Monday
2 What Do I (. . . . .) Back
3 Sabre (. . . . .) Stance
4 New (. . . . .) In The Fast Lane
5 Don't Bring Me Your (. . . . .) By The Number
6 Carolina (. . . . .) Shadow
7 Dippety (. . . . .) Tripper
8 Zipgun (. . . . .) Nights
9 Mystery (. . . . .) To Skaville

10 Because You're (. . . . .) Girl

1 You Can't Be True To (. . . . .) Little Boys
2 Love (. . . . .) Come Away
3 Tomorrow (. . . . .) Sun
4 Finchley (. . . . .) Park Arrest
5 Goodnight (. . . . .) To Six Man
6 Million (. . . . .) Are My Beat
7 Polk Salad (. . . . .) Get Your Gun
8 Helen (. . . . .) Ain't Coming Down
9 Sky (. . . . .) Of The Airwaves
10 Furniture (. . . . .) And Lights

QUIZ 8

YOU'LL ALWAYS FIND ME IN THE KITCHEN AT PARTIES

Score one point for each correct answer.

1 Which song featured the line 'Get out in that kitchen and rattle those pots and pans?'
2 Who drank from the loving cup and found a storm in a teacup?
3 Where did Simon and Garfunkel's Mrs Robinson keep her cup cakes?
4 Which Gilbert O'Sullivan song starts with the line 'Mum the kettle's boiling'?
5 Who found love in a cupboard in 1963?
6 What did Tin Tin have for tea provided by the Bee Gees?
7 Which Top Ten haute cuisine group did magic in 1973 and a miracle in 1974?
8 What would chart topping Eileen Barton have said in 1950 if she knew you were coming?
9 Eileen Barton may have had the 'Just Don't Want To Be Lonely' group as the major part of her gateaux
10 Paul Young made this with the Streetband

<table>
<tr><td>QUIZ 9</td><td>OVER UNDER SIDEWAYS DOWN</td></tr>
</table>

You can remember a lot of the number one hit singles in Britain, but can you remember what was on the other side of all those number ones? In this quiz, we list the titles of the B-sides of 75 number ones over the years, and all you have to do is name the A-side title and artist.

 **A**

1 'Putting On The Style'
2 'Claudette'
3 'Carolina Moon'
4 'I Got Stung'
5 'Brown Girl In The Ring'
6 'Too Shy' (Instrumental)
7 'Little Sister'
8 'Climb Ev'ry Mountain'
9 'Bachelor Boy'
10 'I Need Your Love Tonight'
11 'We Can Work It Out'
12 'Yellow Submarine'
13 'Can't Help Falling In Love'
14 'First Cut Is The Deepest'
15 'Cabaret'
16 'Candy Girl' (Singalong)
17 'Rock Your Baby Part 2'
18 'Puppy Song'
19 'Ebony Eyes'
20 'Precious'
21 'Girl's School'
22 'Computer Love'
23 'I Don't Wanna Dance' (Accapella)
24 'Dreams of Children'
25 'Catch A Falling Star'

 **B**

1 'Lifeline'
2 'Cat People (Putting Out Fire)'
3 'Shopping'
4 'Dub Version (featuring Pappa Weasel)'

18 'Don't Look Back'
19 'Chained'
20 'Red Scab'
21 'Sandy'
22 'Don't Tell Me Tell Her'
23 'Talking' Bout Ya'
24 'Saturday Night Out'
25 'Don't Gamble With Love'

| QUIZ 10 | NUMBER ONE SONG IN HEAVEN |

The following questions all concern records which have reached number one on the American singles chart.

1 Who was Johnny Mathis' partner in a 1978 number one?

2 Who had the number one version of the *Star Wars* theme?

3 David Bowie and John Lennon co-wrote which number one?

4 Four number one singles were taken from the soundtrack to *Saturday Night Fever*. Three were by the Bee Gees. What was the fourth and who was the artist?

5 Otis Redding reached the top with which posthumous release?

6 What number one for Hugh Masekela was later a hit in a vocal version by the Friends of Distinction?

7 Simon and Garfunkel expanded a number from *The Graduate* and took it to number one. What was it?

8 What was the Monkees' longest-running number one?

9 Herb Alpert, normally an instrumentalist, had a number one as a vocalist with a song debuted on the TV special *The Beat of the Brass*. What was it?

10 What number one by Ringo Starr had originally been a hit for Johnny Burnette?

11 Andy Kim co-wrote the number one 'Sugar Sugar'. What was his chart-topper as an artist?

12 Roberta Flack got her breakthrough when Clint Eastwood played her song in *Play Misty For Me*. The record subsequently went to number one. What was it?

13 The Jackson Five had four number ones with their first four Motown releases. What was the first?

14 Which Bobby Darin number one came from *The Threepenny Opera*?

15 George Harrison's 'My Sweet Lord' was musically inspired by what previous number one?

16 What Frankie Valli number one was written by Barry Gibb?

17 B J Thomas made it with what song from *Butch Cassidy and the Sundance Kid*?

18 Smokey Robinson and the Miracles had twenty-five top forty hits before their first number one. What was the chart-topper?

19 Which side of the Beatles' double-sided hit 'Penny Lane/Strawberry Fields Forever' became a US number one?

20 Bobby Vee once recorded a song called 'How Many Tears.' How many tears did ? and the Mysterians sing about on their 1966 number one?

21 Gladys Knight and the Pips took it to number two. Within a year Marvin Gaye took it the extra step. What was it?

22 Irene Cara had a number one in which the title was never sung. What was it?

23 Who was the hero of Jimmy Dean's number one about a coal mining disaster?

24 The first single from the album 'Synchronicity' was number one in America for eight weeks. Who was the artist and what was the record?

25 What was the Animals' only US number one?

26 The theme from *Rocky 3* was a number one. What was the title and who was the artist?

27 Elton John played on which John Lennon number one?

28 John Lennon played on which Elton John number one?

29 The Temptations went to number one with the original version of a song later made famous in Britain by Otis Redding. What was it?

30 What number one was subtitled '(Enough Is Enough)'?

 **B**

1 Peter Wolf sang lead vocal on which number one?

2 What did 'TSOP' stand for?

3 Two former members of the Fifth Dimension reached the top together. Who were they and what was their hit?

4 What was Rose Royce's number one from *Car Wash*?

5 The title of what Barry Manilow number was a fib?

6 John Sebastian scored a solo number one with a TV theme ten years after his last list leader with the Lovin' Spoonful. What was the song?

7 What was Abba's only American number one?

8 In 1968 a Eurovision Song Contest loser became a US number one as an instrumental by Paul Mauriat. What was the song?

9 What number was written as a description of Don McLean's effect on his audience?

10 Henry Mancini's most famous record was 'Moon River.' His only number one, however, was from a film adaptation of a Shakespeare play. What was the record?

11 Paul and Linda McCartney had an American number one never released as a single in Britain, though it did appear in the UK on the album 'Ram'. What was it?

12 The Righteous Brothers had two number ones. What was the first?

13 Elvis Presley paraphrased Shakespeare on which number one?

14 Gene Pitney's 'Only Love Can Break a Heart' got to number two. It was held off number one by a song he had written. Name the record and artist.

15 Who was Soeur Sourire and what was her number one?

16 What Beatles number one was originally conceived by Paul McCartney with John Lennon's son Julian in mind?

17 Gogi Grant had a US number one with a tune that later gave Frank Ifield a British chart topper. What was it?

18 David Seville reached the top with his own hit 'Witch Doctor'. He also made it under a pseudonym. What was the false name and what was the number one?

19 What was Elvis Presley's first US number one?

20 Who said there were two girls for every boy, and where did this phenomenon occur?

21 The Jackson Five had four number ones with their first four Motown releases. What was the third?

22 Diana Ross and the Supremes had the Christmas number one of 1969. What was it?

23 Queen had two number ones from 'The Game'. Name them.

24 Name the two comic book heroes mentioned in Donovan's US number one.

25 What number one song was about a rat?

26 Who recorded a tribute to Duke Ellington and took it to

number one? What was it called?

27 Neil Sedaka reached the Top Ten in 1976 with a ballad version of his 1962 number one. What was the song?

28 What number one was subtitled '(The Pina Colada Song)'?

29 Their Christian names were Denny and Rick and the sub-title of their number one was '(Exordium and Terminus)'. What were their surnames and what was their only hit?

30 In which Supremes number one did Diana Ross name the members of the group?

1 On what number one does a backing singer claim 'Sedaka is back'?

2 Who is Baldemar Huerta and what was his number one?

3 What was the Bay City Rollers' only US number one?

4 What is the only number one to get to the top during each of two completely separate chart runs?

5 In which number one did the singer say "I feel the bullet go deep in my chest"?

6 What was the first American number one by a British artist?

7 Three number ones in a row in 1964 were by the Beatles. Who replaced them and with which song?

8 Who was the lead singer of the Fireballs on their 1963 number one 'Sugar Shack'?

9 What was the only Japanese language US number one?

10 These folk singers came together at Wesleyan University in Connecticut. Who were they and what was their number one?

11 Steve Lawrence had a number one with this song in 1963. What was the song and who had a number one remake of it in 1971?

12 They performed in the film *Beyond the Valley of the Dolls*. Who were they and what was their number one?

13 Who first recorded Chuck Berry's 'My Ding-a-Ling' years before, in 1954?

14 What number one came from the film *Willy Wonka and the Chocolate Factory*? Who was the artist?

15 The mother of one of the *Star Wars* characters recorded which American number one? Who was she?

16 Which American number one was featured in the film *Under Water!*?

17 Perez Prado had a number one in both the US and UK with 'Cherry Pink and Apple Blossom White'. What was his second American number one?

18 On which American number one does a member of the backing band loudly cry out "What key? What key?"?

19 What number one was sung by an artist who subsequently became a popular disc jockey on WNEW-New York?

20 What novelty number one was performed by a man who became a regular in the TV series *Rawhide* and had country hits under the name Ben Colder?

21 Which American number one was one of Princess Margaret's Desert Island Discs?

22 Who had a number one with 'Mr Custer'?

23 Which American number one was written as a warning against alcohol and was the first record to break as a result of heavy TV exposure?

24 What number one was subtitled '(Live at Glasgow)'?

25 What was Robin Scott's number one?

26 Who first recorded 'I Love Rock and Roll', ultimately a number one for Joan Jett and the Blackhearts?

27 B J Thomas had a long-winded title at number one. The parenthetical beginning of it was '(Hey Won't You Play)'. What was the rest of the title?

28 What was the number one by the Fontane Sisters?

29 What was the last number one by the Commodores?

30 Domenico Modugno's number one is well-known as 'Volare'. That was, in fact, the sub-title on the American release. What was the full title?

QUIZ 11 | IT'S ONLY ROCK 'N' ROLL?

Not all the music that makes the charts has its origin in rock or the blues. Classical music and rural folk music has also made an impression both in their original forms and in rock reworkings. The following questions are based on this music.

1 Who held the UK number one spot for six weeks in 1967 with a tune adapted from a Bach composition?

2 The Nice and Captain Sensible share which special distinction?

3　Who took 'Classical Gas' into the top ten in 1968?

4　In 1983 David Essex had a hit with a song from his musical *Mutiny!* What was the song?

5　A note for note, but speeded up version of a piece from 'The Nutcracker Suite' was a number one hit for whom?

6　Sounds Inc. were one of many bands to record a version of the 'Lone Ranger Theme'. Which overture was this based on and who composed it?

7　Thin Lizzy's first hit single, was a reworking of which Irish folk song?

8　Who wrote 'Roll Over Beethoven?'

 **B**

1　In 1969 the Welsh trio Love Sculpture, with Dave Edmunds on lead guitar, released a frantic version of the 'Sabre Dance'. Which classical composer originated it?

2　Which orchestra took 'Hooked On Classics' to number two during the 1981 medley-mania?

3　In 1971 Emerson, Lake and Palmer released a live album based on a classical work by Mussorgsky. What was their album called?

4　Dublin band Horslips based much of their music on traditional Irish folk melodies. Only one of their albums made the UK charts. What was it's full title?

5　Which famous musical were the following songs from; 'Don't Cry For Me Argentina', 'Oh What A Circus', 'Another Suitcase In Another Hall'?

6　Manfred Mann's Earth Band 1973 hit 'Joybringer' was based on which planet's theme from Holst's Planet Suite?

7　Which member of Deep Purple co-wrote, with Malcolm Arnold, 'A Concerto For Group And Orchestra?'

8　Ennio Morricone took the theme from a BBC TV series to number two in 1981. What was the tune called?

 **C**

1　The most surprising number one of 1972 was surely a rendition of a famous Scottish anthem. What was it and who took it to the top?

2　The Electric Light Orchestra's second album was recorded by nine musicians. Six came from various rock bands but three were enlisted from which famous orchestra?

3　In 1976 a guitar concerto made the number one position for a mere three hours after which it was realised a mistake had been made in that week's chart positions.

The record was restored to its correct position of number four and it never climbed higher than three. What was it and by whom?

4   The Cougars only hit was 'Saturday Night At The Duck Pond', a reworking of which piece of ballet music?

5   A pop version of 'Hall of The Mountain King' started with the immortal spoken words, "Say, Brutus Man, Like where is this King's pad?". Who recorded it?

6   Who were the first rock band to play at the London Proms?

7   A group of American classical musicians formed a band as an outlet for pop renditionings of more classically orientated material such as 'Piltdown Rides Again' and 'Goodnight Mrs Flintstone'. Who were they?

8   The Shadows reworked a song more usually associated with the trenches during World War One. What was it?

1 Name the
  batsman. Name
  the fielder. Name
  their
  replacements in
  the team

2 Name the
  trumpeter

3 A camera-shy 60s
  pop star tries to
  conceal himself.
  Do you recognise
  him?

4 Who is this giving
  himself a neck
  massage?

5 Who's hiding
  behind the
  smokescreen of a
  Capstan full
  strength in Bristol?

6 Name the rockin'
violinist

7 Far right: This is
Steve and Rikki.
What is the link
between them
and John, Dec
and Con?

8 Why does this
man possess such
exotic wallpaper?

9 Place the bass face

10 Who is the owner of the gleaming new Austin Healey?

<table>
<tr><td>QUIZ 13</td><td>I WRITE THE SONGS</td></tr>
</table>

The writers of all the songs in this quiz are all well known, and not necessarily only for writing hit records. Who are they?

A

1. 'Jealous Guy', Roxy Music
2. 'The Crown', Gary Byrd
3. 'The First Cut Is The Deepest', Rod Stewart
4. 'Leavin' On A Jet Plane', Peter, Paul and Mary
5. 'Red Red Wine', UB 40
6. 'Bad To Me', Billy J Kramer and the Dakotas
7. 'Baby Come Back', Equals
8. 'Claudette', Everly Brothers
9. 'Wombling Song', Wombles
10. 'A World Without Love', Peter and Gordon
11. 'It Doesn't Matter Anymore', Buddy Holly
12. 'Woodstock', Matthews Southern Comfort
13. 'Mighty Quinn', Manfred Mann
14. 'I'm A Believer', Monkees
15. 'Out Of Time', Chris Farlowe and The Thunderbirds
16. 'All The Young Dudes', Mott The Hoople
17. 'Mr Tambourine Man', Byrds
18. 'Something', Beatles
19. 'Johnny Reggae', Piglets
20. 'Dear Prudence', Siouxsie and the Banshees

B

1. 'Combine Harvester', Wurzels
2. 'Love Me For A Reason', Osmonds
3. 'Puppy Love', Donny Osmond
4. 'San Francisco (Be Sure To Wear Some Flowers In Your Hair)', Scott McKenzie
5. 'Sugar Sugar', Archies
6. 'Long Live Love', Sandie Shaw
7. 'Living Doll', Cliff Richard
8. 'Argentine Melody (Cancion De Argentina)', San Jose
9. 'I'm Into Something Good', Herman's Hermits
10. 'Anyone Who Had A Heart', Cilla Black
11. 'Do You Love Me', Brian Poole and the Tremeloes

12 'Here Comes My Baby', Tremeloes
13 'Wonderful Land', Shadows
14 'Ebony Eyes', Everly Brothers
15 'Woman In Love', Barbra Streisand
16 'The Tide Is High', Blondie
17 'I Wanna Be Your Man', Rolling Stones
18 'Eloise', Barry Ryan
19 'Bright Eyes', Art Garfunkel
20 'All Along The Watchtower', Jimi Hendrix Experience

 C

1 'I Can't Stop Loving You', Ray Charles
2 'Walk Right Back', Everly Brothers
3 'Tobacco Road', Nashville Teens
4 'Do You Mind', Anthony Newley
5 'Sixteen Tons', Tennessee Ernie Ford
6 'Clown Shoes', Johnny Burnette
7 'Blinded By The Light', Manfred Mann's Earth Band
8 'They Don't Know', Tracey Ullman
9 'And I Love You So', Perry Como
10 'Angel', Rod Stewart
11 'Blue Turns To Grey', Cliff Richard
12 'Cinderella Rockefella', Esther and Abi Ofarim
13 'The Puppy Song', David Cassidy
14 'Eve of Destruction', Barry McGuire
15 'Floy Joy', Supremes
16 'Hello Mary Lou', Ricky Nelson
17 'He's A Rebel', Crystals
18 'If I Were A Carpenter', Bobby Darin
19 'It's All Over', Cliff Richard
20 'The Lion Sleeps Tonight', Tight Fit

THREE STEPS TO HEAVEN

The following quiz contains three sets of titles. The same act has recorded each track with the same number . . . for example, the same group has recorded song number 1 in Group A, 1 in Group B, and 1 in Group C.

Your task is to identify the act that has recorded the three tracks. If you can guess the identity from the title listed in Group A, score 3 points. If you need to also look at the title in Group B before making a correct identification, you get 2 points. If it takes you until the last, extremely familiar, title, you score 1 point.

Needless to say, the tracks are arranged in reverse order of familiarity. Only a devotee of the artist is certain to know the track in Group A, while many will know the tracks in Group B and nearly everybody will know the numbers in Group C.

 **A**

1   'Yesterday's Papers'
2   'I've Been Lonely Too Long'
3   'Tell The Children'
4   'Cold Love'
5   'Blue Jay Way'
6   'The Elephant's Graveyard (Guilty)'
7   'Anastasia'
8   'The Girl That Stood Beside Me'
9   'Uptown Festival'
10 'Careless Memories'
11 'In The Stone'
12 'New Morning'
13 'Take My Time'
14 'Superman's Big Sister'
15 'Be Careful Of Stones That You Throw'
16 'I'm In Love (And I Love the Feeling)'
17 'Remembering Marie'
18 'Victim Of Love'
19 'Sweet Cherry Wine'
20 'Morning Glow'
21 'From The Candy Store On The Corner To The Chapel On The Hill'
22 'We Will'
23 'Ride Away'

24 '992 Arguments'
25 'Coconut'
26 'I'm A Woman'
27 'Lovin' Up A Storm'
28 'Didn't You Know (You'd Have to Cry Sometime)'
29 'This Girl Is A Woman Now'
30 'I Won't Close My Eyes'

 **B**

1 'Fool To Cry'
2 'People Got To Be Free'
3 'Angels With Dirty Faces'
4 'Down Deep Inside'
5 'Dr Robert'
6 'Someone's Looking At You'
7 'Moody River'
8 'Multiplication'
9 'The Second Time Around'
10 'My Own Way'
11 'Shining Star'
12 'Can You Please Crawl Out Your Window'
13 'Telefone (Long Distance Love Affair)'
14 'Sweet Gene Vincent'
15 'Donna The Prima Donna'
16 'I Wanna Get Next To You'
17 'Suffragette City'
18 'Crazy Water'
19 'Hanky Panky'
20 'She's Out Of My Life'
21 'The Good Life'
22 'Why Oh Why Oh Why'
23 'Falling'
24 'Used Ta Be My Girl'
25 'Everybody's Talking'
26 'Is That All There Is'
27 'High School Confidential'
28 'If I Were Your Woman'
29 'Woman Woman'
30 'The Earth Dies Screaming'

1 'Honky Tonk Women'
2 'Groovin''
3 'Hersham Boys'
4 'I Feel Love'
5 'She Loves You'
6 'Rat Trap'
7 'Love Letters In The Sand'
8 'Dream Lover'
9 'There It Is'
10 'Hungry Like The Wolf'
11 'After the Love Is Gone'
12 'Like A Rolling Stone'
13 '9 to 5'
14 'Hit Me With Your Rhythm Stick'
15 'The Wanderer'
16 'Car Wash'
17 'Space Oddity'
18 'Your Song'
19 'Mony Mony'
20 'Billie Jean'
21 'I Left My Heart In San Francisco'
22 'Alone Again (Naturally)'
23 'Oh Pretty Woman'
24 'Love Train'
25 'Without You'
26 'Fever'
27 'Great Balls Of Fire'
28 'Midnight Train To Georgia'
29 'Young Girl'
30 'Red Red Wine'

<table>
<tr><td>QUIZ 15</td><td># SILLY LOVE SONGS</td></tr>
</table>

This is a section about recordings that are classified as "Novelty". It's rather hard to define exactly what a novelty recording is, but nearly everything comic and anything with some kind of gimmicky instrumentation or insane lyric qualifies. There are borderline cases such as the magnificent 'YMCA' by the Village People – but no artiste should feel too offended if their work is classified as novelty. The one thing novelty discs always do is entertain, and that is one of the prime aims, nay duties, of anyone committing him/herself to tape.

 **A**

Who gave us these moments to remember? All UK chart hits.
1　'Itsy Bitsy Teeny Weeny Yellow Polka Dot Bikini'
2　'My Boomerang Won't Come Back'
3　'Shaddap You Face'
4　'Save Your Love'
5　'The Laughing Gnome'
6　'Yellow Submarine'
7　'My Ding-A-Ling'
8　'Ernie (The Fastest Milkman In The West)'
9　'D.I.V.O.R.C.E.' (not the original, extremely sincere, version by Tammy Wynette)
10　'Lily The Pink'
11　'Birdie Song (Birdie Dance)'
12　'Da Da Da'
13　'Yummy Yummy Yummy'
14　'Um Um Um Um Um Um'
15　'Telephone Man'

 **B**

1　Which American male vocalist scored his only UK number one with a song about a gentleman who exposed himself in public places?
2　What song of Melanie's did the Wurzels replough as 'Combine Harvester'?
3　Which great British comedy rock group had just one single hit 'I'm The Urban Spaceman' with a serious song?
4　Who had hits in the early sixties with 'Hole In The Ground' and 'Right Said Fred'
5　Who acting whom, reading which Beatles lyric was

impersonated by Peter Sellers on a 1965 hit?

6 Who sang 'Bangers And Mash' with whom?

7 Who had difficulty being served with two pints of lager in 1980?

8 Which comic group include Duke D'Mond in their ranks?

9 Which group now more famous for their impressions and on-stage comedy began their career with several straight pop hits including 'Poor Man's Son'?

10 Which group, once known as Stavely Makepiece, followed up their number one novelty instrumental with a tribute to 'Desperate Dan'?

11 Which bloke sang 'My Girl Bill'?

12 Who were Alvin, Simon, Theodore, Ross, David, Alfi and Harry?

13 Which American country/pop singer wrote 'You Can't Roller Skate In A Buffalo Herd', 'Dang Me' and 'My Uncle Used To Love Me But She Died', and scored his only UK number one with a song about a wandering hobo?

14 What relation is the singer of the 1977 hit version of 'Halfway Down The Stairs' to Kermit The Frog?

15 Which British pianist wrote 'Orville's Song' for Orville and his voice, Keith Harris?

Name the performer and record (some only hits in the US) to which the following novelty or gimmicky ideas brought chart success:

1 A vicious attack on individuals of limited stature

2 Gunfire and name-checks to nearly every cowboy TV series of the day

3 Assorted ghouls dancing

4 A cartoon caveman

5 The union between one of the world's richest and one of bedtime's fairest

6 An extremely long list of recording stars and other music business names

7 A young boy's letter home from holiday camp

8 Glenn Miller plus chickens

9 The economics of animal ownership

10 French passion

11 A famous UK TV commentator/presenter and rap

12 A worker in the farinaceous industry with royal delusions

13 A telephone answering machine
14 A Yuletide request for a moptop
15 A wobbleboard

| QUIZ 16 | SPLISH SPLASH |

Score one point for each correct answer.

1 Who were 'Clean Clean' in 1980?
2 Who had a mirror in their bathroom?
3 What did Showaddywaddy borrow from the Jarmels?
4 What colours were Max's toothbrushes?
5 What unclean vow did the Brook Brothers make?
6 Who peeped through the bathroom door and allegedly saw their sister in the raw in 1971?
7 According to the Beatles how did the girl in Abbey Road get into the bathroom?
8 What would they have called the freshly scrubbed Ray Davies as he emerged from the bathroom?
9 Although there were five of them what did the Equals sing in the tub in 1969?
10 What did the Rockin' Berries sing as they lay in the bath completely covered?

| QUIZ 17 | DEDICATED TO THE ONE I LOVE |

Many hit songs have been about real people, even if they haven't all been tributes. How many do you remember?

1 Who did Danny Mirror remember?
2 Who did Haysi Fantayzee say was big leggy?
3 Who did Mike Berry sing a tribute to?
4 Who did the guy working down the chip shop swear he was?
5 Dexy's Midnight Runners' first number one was about which 1960s London r&b giant?
6 Don McLean's first British number one was about which

nineteenth century painter?

7 Who shared title billing with Martin Luther King and John F Kennedy in Marvin Gaye's 1970 hit?

8 Ennio Morricone's 'Chi Mai' was the theme of a TV series about the life and times of which Prime Minister?

9 Which American gangsters inspired a Georgie Fame number one?

10 Which American gangster inspired a Blue Beat Top 20 hit in 1967 for Prince Buster?

11 Who invented the telephone, and whose song about him hit the Top 40 in 1971?

12 Which South American president's wife asked her country not to cry for her?

13 Whose dream was it that Spurs are on their way to Wembley?

14 Who did Dora Bryan want for Christmas?

15 Who did Heinz want to be just like?

16 Elton John's 'Empty Garden' was a tribute to which of his hit partners?

17 Elton John's 'Candle In The Wind' was about which American film actress?

18 Whose eyes did Kim Carnes accuse the lady of having?

19 Which World War I flying ace's return did the Royal Guardsmen sing about?

20 Roxy Music's 'Jealous Guy' was a tribute to the writer of the song. Who was he?

 **B**

1 Brian and Michael's one-hit wonder chart-topper was about a twentieth century British artist. Which one?

2 Who were the three stars of Ruby Wright's song?

3 Charlie Drake covered an American number one about which nineteenth century American general?

4 Who did Larry Cunningham and the Mighty Avons sing a tribute to?

5 Who was Don Fardon's Belfast boy?

6 For whom was 'Hey Jude' originally written?

7 For whom was 'Annie's Song' written?

8 Who was Cat Stevens' inspiration for his first Island hit?

9 Which King did William Bell sing a tribute to?

10 Who was Stevie Wonder wishing a happy birthday in his hit single of that title?

11 About whom was Joyce Blair's only hit, and under what name did she record it?

12 Who did the Cockerel Chorus consider a nice one?

13 According to 'Creeque Alley' by the Mamas and Papas, who was "just getting higher in L.A. you know where that's at"?

14 Who called John and Yoko to say you can get married in Gibraltar near Spain?

15 Which comedy duo hit number two in the charts 7 years after the Equals hit the charts with a song named for them?

16 Who was George Harrison singing about 'All Those Years Ago'?

17 Whose ballad was a hit for four people in 1956?

18 About whom was 'Killing Me Softly With His Song' written?

19 After whom was Bill Haley's 'Rudy's Rock' named?

20 Who was in a golden coach, according to Billy Cotton's 1953 hit?

 C

1 Who went on the 'Caribbean Honeymoon' that Frank Weir named his 1960 hit after?

2 Who was Gilbert O'Sullivan's Clair?

3 About whom is 'The Folk Singer' generally believed to have been written?

4 Whose career did Bill Parsons' 'All American Boy' deal humourously with?

5 Who was Bob Dylan's Hurricane?

6 What happened on the day Don McLean's music died? What was the 'bad news on the doorstep'?

7 Who was the reet petite star who said things, according to Van Morrison?

8 Who did John Lennon ask 'How Do You Sleep'?

9 For whom was Elton John's 'Song For Guy'?

10 To whom was Neil Sedaka's 'Oh Carol' referring?

11 After whom did Ray Stevens name Ahab the Arab's camel, Clyde?

12 Who is the 'Pops' that Marvin Gaye, Diana Ross, Stevie Wonder and Smokey Robinson said they loved in 1979?

13 In the Four Preps 'More Money For You And Me' hit of 1961, who were "Stealing hub caps off cars"?

14 In 'Have A Drink On Me', Lonnie Donegan claims that you can make more money by writing songs for a certain recording artist than by drilling for oil or panning for gold. Who is the artist?

15 About whom did Orchestral Manoeuvres in the Dark have two hit singles?

16 To which architect did Simon and Garfunkel say "So Long" on 'Bridge Over Troubled Water' LP?

17 To whom was David Parton referring when he sang 'Isn't She Lovely'?

18 The Crosby, Stills, Nash and Young 1971 live album 'Four Way Street' included a song called 'Long Time Gone'. To whom was this song a tribute?

19 Who was the Scotty that Bobby Goldsboro watched grow in the US Top 20 in 1971?

20 Who did Waylon Jennings insist "is still the King" in a hit country single?

<table>
<tr><td>QUIZ 18</td><td># I'M GONNA SIT RIGHT DOWN AND WRITE MYSELF A LETTER</td></tr>
</table>

When filled in properly the squares in the big box spell out a familiar lyric from a popular song. Fill them in by answering clues A through to U. Each letter of each answer corresponds to a square in the big box. For example, the third letter of the answer to clue M belongs in square M3; the fifth letter of the answer to clue B goes in square B5.

After you have filled in quite a few squares in the big box you will be able to guess complete words and, eventually, the entire quotation. This will enable you to fill in the answers to clues you found especially difficult, in reverse fashion.

If this puzzle is to be done in competition with a friend, dare we suggest that you buy another copy of the book. Then see who gets all the correct answers and the complete quotation first. The publishing credit for the lyric is in the answer section.

A   Act that recorded the lyric (7) __ __ __ __ __ __ __

B   The J Geils Band came from this city (6) __ __ __ __ __ __

C   Canadian Scott who sang 'My True Love' (4) __ __ __ __

D   John Lennon's second wife (3) __ __ __

E   Roger, John, Keith and Pete (3,3) __ __ __/__ __ __

F   Summer 1961 hit by Anthony Newley (3,4,3,6) __ __ __/ __ __ __ __/__ __ __/__ __ __ __ __ __

G   __ __ __ __ Cass (4)

H   'It's __ __ __ __ Dad,' 1962 film and top three soundtrack (4)

I   '__/__ __ __/__ __/__ __ __ Life,' last track on 'Sergeant Pepper's Lonely Hearts Club Band' (1,3,2,3)

J   '__ __ __ __ in the Wind,' 1978 Kansas ballad (4)

K   US label, distributed by Atlantic, featuring Joe Tex (4) __ __ __ __

L   '__ __ __ Only Knows,' Beach Boys classic (3)

M   __ __ __ __ __ Master Flash and the Furious Five (5)

N   '__ __ __ __ __/__ __ Me,' Sonny's only solo hit (5,2)

O   '__ __/__ __/__ __ . . .', repetitive beginning of 'O Superman' (2,2,2)

P   '__ __ __/__ __ __ Road Jack,' Ray Charles' first UK top ten hit (3,3)

Q   Jimmy Pursey told him to hurry (5) __ __ __ __ __

R   Pete Wylie's exclamatory group (3) __ __ __!

S   Morning __ __ __,' standard written by Tim Rose (3)

T   '__ __ __/__ __ __ It,' Hurricane Smith's last hit (3,3)

U   One of Wink Martindale's cards, the __ __ __ __ __ (4)

●	●	P2	●	H2	E3	K3	J1	●	U1
N5	F10	●	D2	I9	S3	F7	●	P4	B2
I2	N2	Q5	●	F2	T2	●	A1	L2	I4
●	Q2	B1	E6	J2	N7	●	R2	●	A5
O3	C3	C4	U4	●	G1	A3	I6	●	R1
R3	B5	●	G3	T5	M5	F6	●	I7	E5
F12	●	M1	U2	G4	K1	F15	●	H3	M4
L3	●	B4	Q1	F5	O5	N4	P5	●	P3
O4	S2	●	B6	A6	T4	T6	●	T1	F13
A7	●	Q3	C2	H1	P1	U3	M2	●	F14
N6	H4	●	F11	A2	K4	N1	●	I5	●
C1	O1	J3	E1	●	F9	G2	S1	●	J4
D1	●	F16	I3	N3	F4	E2	●	K2	●
B3	M3	E4	●	F8	O6	P6	●	F1	O2
D3	A4	T3	L1	Q4	I1	F3	I8	●	●

MISSING WORDS

The following song titles are all incomplete. The full titles include brackets which are missing here. Fill in the complete title.

 **A**

1 Eddie Holman – Lonely Girl
2 Steve Harley and Cockney Rebel – Mr Raffles
3 David Bowie – Scary Monsters
4 Rocky Sharpe and the Replays – Shout Shout
5 Haircut 100 – Favourite Shirts
6 Elvis Costello – Chelsea
7 Donna Summer – Love Is In Control
8 Rod Stewart – Tonight I'm Yours
9 Paul Anka – Having My Baby
10 Stevie Wonder – Uptight
11 Edison Lighthouse – Love Grows
12 Barry Blue – On A Saturday Night
13 Dexy's Midnight Runners – Let's Get This Straight
14 Gary Glitter – I Didn't Know I Loved You
15 John Lennon – Starting Over

 **B**

1 Stranglers – Grip
2 Rod Stewart – What Made Milwaukee Famous
3 Patti Smith – Privilege
4 Level 42 – Are You Hearing
5 George Harrison – Give Me Love
6 Alice Cooper – Love At Your Convenience
7 Scott McKenzie – San Francisco
8 Teardrop Explodes – Treason
9 Tottenham Hotspur FA Cup Squad – Ossie's Dream
10 Ruts DC – West One
11 Jackie Wilson – Higher And Higher
12 Q-Tips – S.Y.S.L.J.F.M.
13 Cilla Black – Something Tells Me
14 Brotherhood Of Man – Oh Boy
15 Tweets – The Birdie Song

C

1 Siouxsie and the Banshees – Mittageisen
2 Slade – C'Est La Vie
3 Tom Browne – Fungi Mama
4 Aretha Franklin – Border Song
5 Everly Brothers – So Sad
6 Perry Como – Hot Diggity
7 Johnny Rivers – Muddy Water
8 Chuck Berry – Nadine
9 Delfonics – Ready Or Not Here I Come
10 Shirley Bassey – I
11 Mindbenders – Can't Live With You
12 Cliff Richard – Wind Me Up
13 Third World – Dancing On the Floor
14 Thin Lizzy – Dancin' In The Moonlight
15 53rd And A 3rd – Chick A Boom

| QUIZ 20 | WORKING ON A BUILDING OF LOVE |

A

1 Whose debut album featured the track 'Bricks And Mortar'?
2 What was Fairport Convention's long playing method of building in 1969?
3 Faron Young said hello to them in the early 60's
4 David Whitfield sang about this internationally famous Italian span in 1953
5 Which ex-Ultravox member used an underpass?
6 The bricks in Pink Floyd's wall kept them higher than anyone else for 5 weeks. Who knocked them down?
7 A 1965 chart topper had some good ingredients for a wall or a bridge – so good they were used again to great effect in 1976. What were they?
8 How many weeks did Simon and Garfunkel's 'Bridge Over Troubled Water' spend at number one? a) 32, b) 36, c) 41
9 In Jimmy Dean's 1962 song who were working on a bridge to cross that water?
10 Which group evolved from the Garden Wall?

QUIZ 21	COME TOGETHER

There are connections between all sorts of unlikely people in the record and charts business, for all sorts of unlikely reasons. This quiz asks you to find out the connections between all sorts of people who might not appear at first glance to be connected.

In Section A, we ask you to put the names of recording acts into the blanks, so that the whole paragraph makes sense. In Section B, we ask you to find the connection between various people, a connection that might be obscure, like shared birthdays, or very obvious, like the connection between George Harrison and Paul McCartney, which we defy anybody to get wrong.

 **A**

. . . . . recorded 'Fool If You Think It's Over', written by . . . . . who had a hit with a song called 'Loving You'. This title was also used by . . . . . who took this, her only hit, to number two in UK . . . . . also had only one British hit, a number two. Their instrumental hit was taken to the edge of the British Top 20 in a vocal version by . . . . . Another person who took a vocal version of a previous instrumental hit into the charts was . . . . . , who also had a hit with 'Let Me Go Lover', which had once been the first British hit for . . . . . This person recorded for the same American label as . . . . . whose 'Words Of Love' was an album track for . . . . . . The brother of one of their members was in another chart-topping group, ... , which split up. Eventually one of the three members briefly joined the one-hit TV group . . . . . . Their hit contained the word 'Bucket' in the title, as did one track on a chart-topping EP by . . . . . . When this group split up, three of their members formed . . . . . , and had a big hit with the standard 'Summertime'. This had earlier been a hit for . . . . . , who was top of the very first chart of all. He starred in an Oscar-winning film whose theme was a hit for . . . . . Another star of this film was Talia Shire, who also starred in three films with the director of *Staying Alive*. The third of these films provided a number one hit for . . . . . . One member of this band had been in the 1970 hit group . . . . . , which was the date Julius Caesar was assassinated.

What is the connection between the following?

 B

1   Nat King Cole and Harry Secombe
2   Harry Secombe and Petula Clark
3   Petula Clark and Anthony Newley
4   Anthony Newley and Cliff Richard
5   Cliff Richard and Buddy Holly
6   Buddy Holly and Mike Berry
7   Mike Berry and Wendy Richard
8   Wendy Richard and Mike Sarne
9   Mike Sarne and Billie Davis
10 Billie Davis and the Exciters
11 The Exciters and Manfred Mann
12 Manfred Mann and Bob Dylan
13 Bob Dylan and George Harrison
14 George Harrison and Paul McCartney
15 Paul McCartney and Stevie Wonder
16 Stevie Wonder and Syreeta Wright
17 Syreeta Wright and Billy Preston
18 Billy Preston and Herb Alpert
19 Herb Alpert and Carly Simon
20 Carly Simon and James Taylor
21 James Taylor and Carole King
22 Carole King and Neil Sedaka
23 Neil Sedaka and the Captain and Tennille
24 Captain and Tennille and the Everly Brothers
25 Everly Brothers and Perry Como
26 Perry Como and Don McLean
27 Don McLean and Roy Orbison
28 Roy Orbison and Glen Campbell
29 Glen Campbell and Conway Twitty
30 Conway Twitty and Barry Gibb
31 Barry Gibb and Frankie Valli
32 Frankie Valli and the Four Seasons
33 Four Seasons and Terry Jacks
34 Terry Jacks and the Poppy Family
35 Poppy Family and Paper Lace
36 Paper Lace and Nottingham Forest FC
37 Nottingham Forest FC and Laurie London

38 Laurie London and Vera Lynn
39 Vera Lynn and Eddie Calvert
40 Eddie Calvert and the Piranhas
41 Piranhas and Lou Busch
42 Lou Busch and Joe 'Fingers' Carr
43 Joe 'Fingers' Carr and Colin Blunstone
44 Colin Blunstone and the Zombies
45 Zombies and Argent
46 Argent and the Bee Gees
47 Bee Gees and Dionne Warwick
48 Dionne Warwick and San Jose
49 San Jose and Jeff Wayne
50 Jeff Wayne and David Essex
51 David Essex and Nat King Cole

Which brings us back to where we started.

QUIZ 22	I'M IN THE MOOD FOR DANCING

The following song titles either mention dancing or name a specific dance. Name the artist who recorded each song.

If you get them all, consider yourself eligible for a life membership at the discotheque of your choice.

1   'Dance Away'
2   'Save The Last Dance For Me'
3   'Dance To The Music'
4   'Let's Dance' (1962)
5   'Let's Dance' (1983)
6   'The Safety Dance'
7   'Land Of 1000 Dances'
8   'He's The Greatest Dancer'
9   'Dancing In The City'
10 'Dancing In The Street'
11 'Dancing Queen'
12 'The Twist' (1962 hit version)
13 'Twistin' The Night Away'

11 'Twine Time'

12 'C'mon And Swim'

13 'Monkey Time'

14 'Hitch Hike'

15 'Tea For Two Cha Cha'

16 'Do The Bird'

17 'Bossa Nova Baby'

18 'Do The Spanish Hustle'

19 'Come To The Dance'

20 'Come On Dance Dance'

QUIZ 23	ONE AND ONE IS ONE

If you take a hit from each of the first two groups below and put them together you will get the title of a hit by the third group shown.

1 McGuire Sisters + David Bowie = Stranglers

2 Rolling Stones + Dusty Springfield = Joan Baez

3 Rolling Stones + Cars = Tommy Steele

4 Don McLean + Roxy Music = Ken Boothe

5 Manhattans + Roy Orbison = Susan Cadogan

6 Split Enz + Styx = Sonny and Cher

7 Cliff Richard + Demis Roussos = Jim Reeves

8 Crystals + Anthony Newley = Showaddywaddy

9 Vardis + Ottowan = Real Thing

10 Eddie Cochran + Kinks = Bee Gees

11 Olivia Newton-John + Lori and the Chameleons = Odyssey

12 Rosemary Clooney + Chris Farlowe = Elvis Costello

13 Flying Lizards + Bobby Goldsboro = Bay City Rollers

14 Elvis Presley + Chordettes = Millie

15 Four Seasons + Peggy Lee = Bee Gees

1 Rolling Stones + Rachel Sweet = Helen Reddy

2 Boney M + Lulu = Don Farden

3 Gerry Monroe + Gene Vincent = David Whitfield

4 Elvis Presley + Barbara Dickson = Cilla Black

5   Gilbert O' Sullivan + Move = KC and the Sunshine Band
6   Darts + P J Proby = Crispy and Company
7   Fleetwood Mac + John Lennon = Brian Hyland
8   Roy Orbison + Zaine Griff = Eagles
9   Osmonds + Minnie Riperton = Ray Charles
10 Telly Savalas + Vernon Girls = Neil Diamond
11 Elvis Presley + Craig Douglas = Fatback Band
12 David Essex + CCS = Chequers
13 Dexy's Midnight Runners + St Louis Union = Herman's Hermits
14 P J Proby + Cliff Richard = Gene Pitney
15 Soft Cell + Val Doonican = Adam Faith

 C

1   Mud + Geno Washington = Elton John
2   Don McLean + Tymes = Sly and the Family Stone
3   Connie Francis + Michael Holliday = Hamilton, Joe Frank and Reynolds
4   Roy Orbison + Paul Anka = Clodagh Rodgers
5   Rita Pavone + Toys = Olivia Newton John
6   Bachelors + George Harrison = Dorothy Moore
7   Rock Candy + Kalin Twins = Platters
8   Jam + Brass Construction = Terry Dene
9   Buster + Truth = Blondie
10 Elvis Presley + Bill Forbes = Specials
11 George Harrison + Buzzcocks = Diana Ross and Marvin Gaye
12 Randy Edelman + Wings = Frank Sinatra
13 Ronettes + Julie Covington, Rula Lenska, Charlotte Cornwell and Sue-Jones Davies = Kenny
14 Herman's Hermits + Junior = Wayne Fontana and the Mindbenders
15 Thom Pace + Perry Como = Lesley Gore

QUIZ 24	ON THE STREET WHERE YOU LIVE

1 Who lived at '461 Ocean Boulevard'?
2 What did they build in Heartache Avenue in 1982/83?
3 Where did Rosemary Clooney, Shakin' Stevens and Billie Anthony live?
4 Where were Heaven 17 inside and outside at the same time in 1981?
5 Which Monaco lady won the Eurovision Song Contest singing about a bench, a tree and a street?
6 Which Australian thoroughfare did the Bee Gees sing about?
7 What was Gene Pitney's 1973 address?
8 Did Liverpudlian coppers live down this narrow track?
9 In 1968 the Move picked their way down here to number one.
10 Who originally sang "in the shadow of a street lamp I turned my collar to the cold and damp"?

QUIZ 25	ALTERNATE TITLE

Many songs have been variations on other songs, translations from other languages or answers to other hits. This quiz is designed to test your knowledge of these spin-off hits.

1 Under what title did the Beach Boys hit with a Crystals smash of four years earlier?
2 Fourteen years after that, Gary Glitter took the same song back into the British charts. What title did he use?
3 What happened to Peggy Sue in Buddy Holly's second hit about that lady?
4 Lydia Murdock's late 1983 hit 'Superstar' was in answer to which earlier number one?
5 On what song was the Wurzels' number one 'Combine Harvester' based?
6 John Fred and the Playboy Band's 1968 hit 'Judy In Disguise (With Glasses)' took its title from which famous LP track?

7 Karl Denver's 'Wimoweh' was based on a South African folk song. Which other song based on the same folk song has been a British hit three times, including one version at number one?

8 What did Jeanne Black answer to Jim Reeves' 'He'll Have To Go'?

9 Chuck Berry's 'No Particular Place To Go' used the same tune as one of his earlier hits. Which one?

10 What was 'I'd Like To Teach The World To Sing' originally titled?

 **B**

1 Under what title did the Beach Boys revive Lonnie Donegan's 1960 top tenner 'I Wanna Go Home'?

2 What tune was the basis for the Springfields' 'Island Of Dreams'?

3 Of which vocal hit was 'Love At First Sight' the instrumental version?

4 Some artists have recorded thematic follow-ups to earlier hits. For example, David Bowie's 'Ashes To Ashes' continued the story of Major Tom, begun in 'Space Oddity'. What was Paul Anka's spin-off hit from an earlier success?

5 And what was Johnny Burnette's?

6 And what was Marty Robbins'?

7 And Lesley Gore's?

8 Scott English's only hit 'Brandy' reappeared in the British charts four years later. Under what title, and by whom?

9 Under what title did the German song 'Moritat' reach number one in Britain, and by whom? Under what other title is the song also well known?

10 Which Elvis Presley number one was an adaptation of the old German folk song, 'Muss I Denn'?

 **C**

1 What was the original French title of Winifred Atwell's number one hit 'Poor People Of Paris'?

2 What was Michael Cox's spin-off hit from an earlier success?

3 Which Elvis Presley number one was based on the old French tune 'Plaisir d'Amour'?

4 What was the English title of the Swedish song 'Ann-Caroline', and who took it to number one?

5 What was the original title of the Monkees' 'Alternate Title'?

6 Whose English version of 'Io Che No Vivo (Senza Te)'

was a number one hit? Under what title?

7 There were many versions of 'I'll Save The Last Dance For You' in answer to the Drifters' 'Save The Last Dance For Me'. But what was the title of Billy Fury's answer to the answer, which was never released as a single?

8 Who recorded the original version of Toni Basil's 'Mickey', and under what title?

9 On which two songs was Billy Connolly's pastiche 'In The Brownies' based?

10 'My Sweet Lord' was not the only track on George Harrison's 'All Things Must Pass' album to run into copyright difficulties. On which copyrighted song was 'It's Johnny's Birthday' based?

| QUIZ 26 | GAYE |

Across

1 'Your . . . . . Love', Marvin and Tammi's biggest US hit. (8)

5 Spandau Ballet song mentioning Mr Gaye . . . . . (4)

7 1966 single by Tommy Roe – 'Sweet . . . . .' (3)

8 Down on one bended . . . . ., classic soul stage stance. (4)

9 'The . . . . . of the City', classic Charlie Gillett r&b book. (5)

11 '. . . . . Da Da', Trio's 1982 smash. (2)

12 '. . . . . See Clearly Now', Johnny Nash 1972 world hit. (1,4)

16 'Look . . . . .', first request in Mathis' 'Misty'. (2,2)

17 'You . . . . . Love to Ball', controversial single from 'Let's Get It On'. (4)

18 It took Marvin and Kim Weston this many. (3)

19 '. . . . . It Baby', Gaye single penned by Berry Gordy. (3)

20 First word in Culture Club's first hit. (2)

21 'I Go . . . . .', Neil Sedaka's gorilla of a hit. (3)

22 '. . . . . The Ladder To The Roof', first Supremes hit without Diana. (2)

23 1979 hit by Kate Bush. (3)

25 David Bowie had a lot of this in his 1980 number one. (3)

26 Science magazine which began publication during Marvin's second decade of hit-making. (4)

27 '. . . . . Shame', Detroit Spinners charter penned by Wonder. (3,1)

29 Artist who originated Gaye's 'Abraham Martin and John'. (4)

30 Three of these gave Wings their hello to the top five. (2)

31 'How . . . . . It Is', Marvin's UK chart debut as soloist. (5)

32 '. . . . . Til' My Bobby Gets Home', Darlene Love threat. (4)

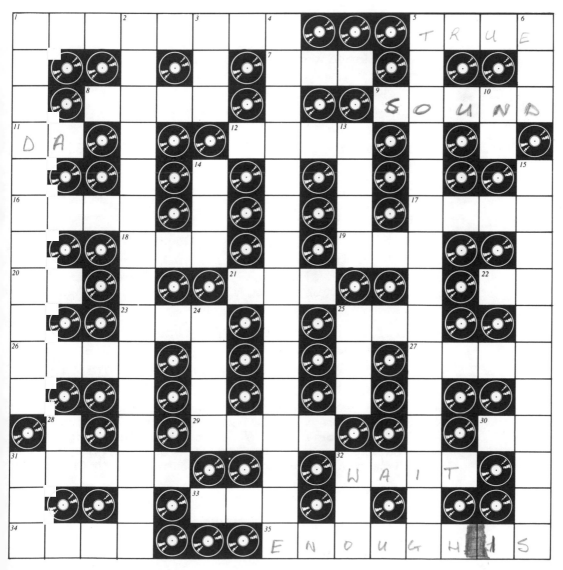

33 Rupert Holmes' follow-up to 'Escape (The Pina Colada Song)'. (3)

34 Gaye's 1974 chart partner. (4)

35 '. . . . . Enough', Streisand and Summer's sentiment. (6,2)

Down

1 Marvin's first US top tenner, a very happy title. (5,3,3)

2 Questioning 1963 classic answered by the Rolling Stones. (3,1,3,1,7)

3 'You're A Wonderful . . . . .', 1964 Gaye release. (3)

4 First single issued by the Marvin-Diana duo, 'You're A . . . . .'. (7,4,2,2)

5 What Marvin was doing about his baby in 1969. (3,4,8)

6 'The . . . . . Of Our Road', Gaye effort also recorded by Gladys Knight and the Pips. (3)

10 A nonsense syllable, but no nonsense for Steam and Bananarama. (2)

13 'I Can't Get . . . . . to You', US number one for 15 Down. (4)

14 Yoko. (3)

15 Group who shared producer Norman Whitfield with Marvin in 1969. (11)

24 Gogi Grant's was wayward and David Bowie's was wild. (4)

25 'You're . . . . . 'I Need To Get By', Gaye-Terrell classic. (3)

28 A 50000 watt radio station has 50 of this (abbreviation). (2)

31 'To . . . . . With Love', unusual Al Green cover of Lulu standard. (3)

32 '. . . . . really cares?' Marvin's first query in 'Save the Children'. (4)

Many of the clues in this crossword deal with the career of Marvin Gaye. Those who know nothing about this legendary Tamla star are in big trouble. We suggest that, if competing against friends, you get another copy of the book and give yourself one point for each square of the puzzle correctly filled in.

<table>
<tr><td>QUIZ 27</td><td># WE DON'T TALK ANYMORE</td></tr>
</table>

These quizzes are all related to instrumental recordings – you know, the ones without words. Actually some instrumentals do have the odd word here and there, but generally these are merely grunts and groans, yells of enthusiasm or at best the title pronounced in a murky tone, which should not be allowed to deny a recording instrumental status. The Shadows are not the answer to every question.

Who had the biggest hit in the UK with the following instrumental tracks?

 **A**

1 'FBI'
2 'Side Saddle'
3 'Tequila'
4 'Eye Level'
5 'Song For Guy'
6 'Don't Cry For Me Argentina'
7 'Telstar'
8 'Wonderful Land'
9 'Nut Rocker'
10 'The Return Of The Los Palmas Seven'
11 'Tubular Bells'
12 'Hoots Mon'
13 'Chariots Of Fire'
14 'Star Wars Theme/Cantina Band'
15 'Albatross'

And with these?

 **B**

1 'Walk Don't Run'
2 'Mouldy Old Dough'
3 'Shindig'
4 'Exodus'
5 'Raunchy'
6 '40 Miles Of Bad Road'
7 'Snow Coach'
8 'Cherry Pink And Apple Blossom White'
9 'A Walk In The Black Forest'
10 'Zorba's Dance'
11 'The Crunch'

12 'Sylvia'

13 'Hooked On Classics'

14 'Chi Mai'

15 'Fanfare For The Common Man'

 C

1 Whose brother took 'Frankenstein' to number one in the States and into the Top 20 in the UK?

2 What is the title of the number 30 UK hit by a top US instrumental combo that has become famous in Britain as the theme for televised cricket?

3 What is the name of the top British orchestra leader who sometimes records as Manuel and his Music of the Mountains?

4 Which two pianists have had two number one hit records in the UK?

5 Cat Stevens had an instrumental hit in the US in 1977/78. Was it called:
(a) 'Was Dog A Doughnut' (b) 'Was God A Doughnut' (c) 'Lady d'Arbanville' (d) 'Was Dog God' (e) 'Walking My Cat Named Dog' (f) He never had a non-vocal hit and this is a trick question?

6 Which famous vocal/instrumental group from Georgia scored an instrumental success in their homeland with 'Jessica'?

7 Which Swedish instrumental group had 4 UK hits including 'Hava Nagila' and 'Orange Blossom Special'?

8 Which British jazzmen scored simultaneous major hits in the US two years before Beatlemania struck over there?

9 And what were the titles of their hits?

10 Which British trombonist had a top Five record on both sides of the Atlantic without having to take his trombone out of its case, and why?

11 Which French instrumental act had their only UK hit in 1977 with a number dedicated to a supernatural insect?

12 What was the title of the Beatles' instrumental track on their 'Magical Mystery Tour' double EP?

13 What was the title of the reggae classic that was a hit twice for Harry J All Stars, in both 1969 and 1980?

14 Which Clint Eastwood movie provided which orchestra with a number one UK smash in 1968?

15 At the time of the setting of this quiz, over ten years have passed since an instrumental record hit number one in the UK. What was the act that achieved this feat in 1973, and what was the name of the tune?

THE WORKER

1   Who originally sang 'Get A Job'?
2   What did Bobby Darin, Tim Hardin and the Four Tops want to be?
3   Which Merseybeat group sang the song 'Milkman'?
4   Who was Ernie the milkman's rival in the Benny Hill chart topper and what was his occupation?
5   What was Sam Cooke working on in 1960?
6   When in 1978 the driver of car 27 refused to pick up his passenger, which other car was offered the job?
7   Duane Eddy's 1959 hit 'Cannonball' coincided with a TV series of the same name. What was the main character's occupation?
8   What was the occupation of the late Alan Smethurst?
9   He had a driving ambition to be on a Duran Duran album.
10   Whistling Jack Smith's temporary occupation in 1967.

QUIZ 29

LIFE IS A LONG SONG

This is where we test your intellectual capabilities. Listed below are forty or so clues, each one leading to the title of a hit single. When all the titles are put together in the order given, then they turn in to a complete, if rather short, story. But that is not all. The first word of the answers to the clues marked with an asterisk * form the letters of the name of the recording act that hit with the answer to the clue marked #. To solve the whole puzzle, you need the complete story and the name of the artist spelt out by the * clues. You may find that the use of a *Guinness Book of British Hit Singles* is essential to find all the answers. So go out and buy one first.

Mott The Hoople's Bowie hit/ Keith's follow up to '98.6'/ Gary Glitter's first number one. Hit title for Frankie Vaughan and also The New Seekers/ Frankie Lymon And The Teenagers second hit/ Clarence 'Frogman' Henry's number three hit/ Kleeer's only 1981 chart entry/ The Kalin Twins' one hit/ Shaky number two between two number ones. The other side of the Frogman's 'Lonely Street'/ the ninth BCR Top

Tenner. Hot Chocolate's only Top Ten hit between 1978 and 1982 */Neil Sedaka's first hit/ Richard Perry's first number one production #. The Merseybeat's smallest hit */ Go-Feet Feet 16/ Eric Clapton's Bob Marley hit*/ a Drifters hit in 65 and 72/ Mike Sarne's motorcycle hit. Val Doonican's shortest hit title */ R Dean Taylor's 1971 Top Tenner/ the final 1982 hit for the 'Red Red Wine' Chart toppers./ Roy Orbison's biggest 1961 hit. Altered Images Xmas 81 smash/ P J Proby's first *West Side Story* hit */ Tracey Ullman's second Top Ten hit/ The final Top Tenner for the Trems. Follow-up to 'The Day The Rains Came'/ Mike Preston's second Top 30 hit/ Jackie Wilson's triple chart entry in 1958. The other side of 'Do You Wanna Dance' on Columbia DB 4828/ Elvis' Stiff hit/ Robert Palmer's biggest before 'Some Guys Have All The Luck'. Johnny Nash's American number one/ Pigmeat Markham and Shorty Long hit title. Fleetwood Mac's first Reprise hit */ Rainbow's early 81 number three hit. The Chiffon's last hit for 3 years until 'Sweet Talking Guy'/ Trems sing Dylan.

| QUIZ 30 | YEARS MAY COME, YEARS MAY GO |

In which year did each of the following events occur?

1 Elvis Presley scores his first hit in the pop charts
2 The Woodstock Music and Arts Fair is held and immediately becomes the most famous rock festival
3 The Beatles release 'Sergeant Pepper's Lonely Hearts Club Band'
4 The Sex Pistols make their chart debut
5 *Saturday Night Fever* sweeps the world
6 Al Martino tops the first singles chart
7 'Rock Around The Clock' becomes the first Rock 'n' Roll number one in both Britain and America
8 A plane crash takes the lives of Buddy Holly, the Big Bopper and Ritchie Valens
9 Dire Straits and Duran Duran perform in front of Prince Charles and Diana, Princess of Wales
10 Fleetwood Mac have America's number one album of the year
11 The summer months become known as the summer of peace and love
12 The Beatles announce their split

13 Elvis Presley dies

14 Slade have three singles enter at number one

15 'Come On Eileen' by Dexy's Midnight Runners is the year's best-selling single

16 John Lennon has his first number one as a soloist

17 Britain's best-selling album of the 1970s is released

18 Diana Ross and the Supremes both appear in the chart for the first time since their separation

19 John Travolta and Olivia Newton-John have two number ones from the *Grease* soundtrack

20 The Apple label is introduced

 B

1 The Police get their first number one

2 'Stairway To Heaven' is released on LP

3 The Beatles first appear on The Ed Sullivan Show

4 Bob Dylan releases his "electric" album 'Highway 61 Revisited'

5 The Supremes go to the top with 'Baby Love'

6 Brian Jones dies

7 'Bright Eyes' is the year's number one

8 Virgin Records debuts with Mike Oldfield's 'Tubular Bells'

9 'Space Oddity' goes to number one on re-issue

10 The Rolling Stones issue their first disc on their own label

11 Two different records based on the *Laugh-In* catch phrase 'Here Comes The Judge' both make the Top 30

12 The first New Wave number one single is achieved

13 The first New Wave number one album is achieved

14 Only the Beatles and Rolling Stones top the LP chart in the whole year

15 'I Hear You Knocking' by Dave Edmunds leaps from sixteen to one

16 Gerry and the Pacemakers have three consecutive number ones with their first three releases

17 The Frank Chacksfield Orchestra has four runs at number two with the same record

18 Louis Armstrong replaces Cliff Richard at number one

19 The Jam reach the Top Ten for the first time

20 Bobby Darin has two straight number ones

1 Cliff Richard has his first year since 1958 without a chart single

2 Freddie Cannon interrupts the run of 'South Pacific' at number one in the album chart

3 Joe Tex dies

4 Steve Strange appears in a David Bowie video

5 Frank Sinatra has his first number one

6 Pat Boone last appears in the Top Ten

7 Bob Marley and the Wailers are recorded live in concert at the Lyceum in London

8 Ruby Murray has seven Top Ten hits

9 Elton John records a song the title of which is his middle name

10 Sir Winston Churchill has a posthumous Top Ten LP

11 The first number one TV soundtrack is achieved

12 Tim Hardin has his only chart single

13 Massiel wins the Eurovision Song Contest

14 One-hit wonders The Dreamweavers have their number one

15 'Amazing Grace' by Judy Collins falls out of the chart for the eighth and final time

16 Elvis Presley has only one week in the album chart all year, that with the soundtrack to *Clambake*

17 The Lovin' Spoonful disband and John Sebastian goes solo

18 Connie Francis has a hit called 'Robot Man'

19 'The Black and White Minstrel Show' is the only album to appear in the LP chart every week of the year

20 The husband and wife team of Rosemary Clooney and José Ferrer both make the Top Ten with two sides of the same single

QUIZ 31	CHAINS

This is an adaptation of the Come Together quiz in this book. Both sections deal with various connections between people, songs, etc.

Who played or sang in both the following acts:

 **A**

1 Manfred Mann and Cream
2 Cream and the Yardbirds
3 The Yardbirds and the Jeff Beck Group
4 Jeff Beck Group and the Faces
5 Faces and Free
6 Free and Bad Company
7 Bad Company and King Crimson
8 King Crimson and Roxy Music
9 Roxy Music and the Nice
10 The Nice and Emerson, Lake and Palmer
11 Emerson, Lake and Palmer and Atomic Rooster
12 Atomic Rooster and Colosseum
13 Colosseum and Rainbow
14 Rainbow and the Outlaws
15 The Outlaws and Hot Chocolate

What is the connection between the following pairs of acts.

 **B**

1 Olivia Newton-John and Electric Light Orchestra
2 Electric Light Orchestra and the Move
3 The Move and Brown Sauce
4 Brown Sauce and Tony Blackburn
5 Tony Blackburn and Elvis Presley
6 Elvis Presley and Floyd Cramer
7 Floyd Cramer and the Shadows
8 The Shadows and the Drifters
9 The Drifters and Engelbert Humperdinck
10 Engelbert Humperdinck and Shakin' Stevens
11 Shakin' Stevens and Pinkerton's Assorted Colours
12 Pinkerton's Assorted Colours and Dollar
13 Dollar and the Beatles

14 Beatles and Mick Jagger
15 Mick Jagger and Peter Tosh
16 Peter Tosh and Chuck Berry
17 Chuck Berry and People's Choice
18 People's Choice and the Three Degrees
19 Three Degrees and Duran Duran
20 Duran Duran and Landscape
21 Landscape and Smokey Robinson and the Miracles
22 Smokey Robinson and the Miracles and the Beat
23 The Beat and Madness
24 Madness and Motorhead
25 Motorhead and Girlschool
26 Girlschool and Gun
27 Gun and Love Sculpture
28 Love Sculpture and Dave Edmunds
29 Dave Edmunds and John Travolta
30 John Travolta and Olivia Newton-John

Now use Olivia to return to the beginning and answer those you couldn't answer first time.

QUIZ 32	WHO AM I

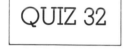

1 ELO – Mr . . . . .
2 Byrds – Mr . . . . .
3 Bert Weedon – Mr . . . . .
4 Keith Relf – Mr . . . . .
5 Ozzy Osbourne's Blizzard of Oz – Mr . . . . .
6 Johnny Cymbal – Mr . . . . .
7 Chordettes – Mr . . . . .
8 Steve Harley and Cockney Rebel – Mr . . . . . , and Mr . . . . .
9 Carpenters – Mr . . . . .
10 Dozy, Beaky, Mick and Tich – Mr . . . . .

<table>
<tr><td></td><td>QUIZ 33</td><td>LET THERE BE DRUMS</td></tr>
</table>

Who played drums on:

A

1 'She Loves You', The Beatles
2 'Satisfaction', The Rolling Stones
3 'Is There Something I Should Know?', Duran Duran
4 'My Generation', Who
5 'Bohemian Rhapsody', Queen
6 'I'm Alive', Hollies
7 'Roxanne', Police
8 'Glad All Over', Dave Clark Five
9 'Apache', Shadows
10 'Don't Cry For Me Argentina', Shadows
11 'That'll Be The Day', Crickets
12 'Going Underground', Jam
13 'Albatross', Fleetwood Mac
14 'Hey Joe', Jimi Hendrix Experience
15 'Jailhouse Rock', Elvis Presley
16 '10538 Overture', Electric Light Orchestra
17 'Blackberry Way', Move
18 'Time (Clock Of The Heart)', Culture Club
19 'I Feel Free', Cream
20 'Uncle Albert/Admiral Halsey', Paul McCartney

B

1 'Picture This', Blondie
2 'Candle In The Wind', Elton John
3 'How Do You Do It', Gerry and The Pacemakers
4 'Needles And Pins', Searchers
5 'You Really Got Me', Kinks
6 'Do Wah Diddy Diddy', Manfred Mann
7 'For Your Love', Yardbirds
8 'Keep On Running', Spencer Davis Group
9 'Bend It', Dave Dee, Dozy, Beaky, Mick and Tich
10 'Do You Love Me', Brian Poole and the Tremeloes
11 'She's Not There', Zombies
12 'I'm The Urban Spaceman', Bonzo Dog Doo Dah Band
13 'Strangers In The Night', Frank Sinatra

and 'Mr Tambourine Man', Byrds

14 'Bridge Over Troubled Water', Simon and Garfunkel
   and 'California Dreamin' ', Mamas and Papas

15 'Rag Mama Rag', The Band

16 'Proud Mary', Creedence Clearwater Revival

17 'Too Shy', Kajagoogoo

18 'Brass In Pocket', Pretenders

19 'House Of The Rising Sun', Animals

20 'Tainted Love', Soft Cell

 C

1 'Like A Rolling Stone', Bob Dylan

2 'Out Of Time', Chris Farlowe

3 'Tragedy', Bee Gees

4 'You've Lost That Lovin' Feelin' ', Righteous Brothers

5 'Wherever I Lay My Hat', Paul Young

6 'Take A Chance On Me', Abba

7 'Ashes To Ashes', David Bowie

8 'Wuthering Heights', Kate Bush
   and '(Come Up And See Me) Make Me Smile', Steve
   Harley and Cockney Rebel

9 'Layla', Derek and the Dominoes

10 'Me And Bobby McGee', Janis Joplin

11 'When I Need You', Leo Sayer
   and 'Empty Garden', Elton John
   and 'The Girl Is Mine', Michael Jackson and Paul
   McCartney

12 'Rock Around The Clock', Bill Haley and his Comets

13 'It's Now Or Never', Elvis Presley

14 'You're Driving Me Crazy', Temperance Seven

15 'Maggie May', Rod Stewart

16 'The Letter', Joe Cocker

17 'Sherry', Four Seasons

18 'December '63 (Oh What A Night)', Four Seasons

19 'Ballad Of John And Yoko', Beatles

20 'Telstar', Tornados

CALL UP THE GROUPS

The following artists all charted in partnership with groups who were credited on the record label. Your job is to complete the name of the act. For example, Al Hudson and the Partners had a Top 20 hit in 1979. If the name Al Hudson appeared below, the correct answer would be 'the Partners.'

1   Father Abraham and the
2   Adam and the
3   Herb Alpert and the
4   Archie Bell and the
5   Big Brother and the
6   Booker T and the
7   Elvis Costello and the
8   Kid Creole and the
9   Terry Dactyl and the
10 Danny and the
11 Desmond Dekker and the
12 Derek and the
13 Dion and the
14 Ian Dury and the
15 Echo and the
16 Wayne Fontana and the
17 Emile Ford and the
18 John Fred and the
19 Gerry and the
20 Grand Master Flash and the
21 Bill Haley and his
22 Steve Harley and
23 Buddy Holly and the
24 Tommy James and the
25 Joan Jett and the
26 Country Joe and the
27 KC and the
28 Johnny Kidd and the
29 Gladys Knight and the
30 Kool and the
31 Billy J Kramer and the

32 Frankie Lymon and the
33 Mamas and the
34 Bob Marley and the
35 Harold Melvin and the
36 Graham Parker and the
37 Tom Petty and the
38 Brian Poole and the
39 Gary Puckett and the
40 Martha Reeves and the
41 Jonathan Richman and the
42 Smokey Robinson and the
43 Kenny Rogers and the
44 Diana Ross and the
45 Bob Seger and the
46 Rocky Sharpe and the
47 Sly and the
48 Bob B Soxx and the
49 Rod Stewart and the
50 Junior Walker and the

 **B**

1 Africa Bambaata and the
2 Alberto y
3 Captain Beefheart and his
4 Hank Ballard and the
5 B Bumble and the
6 Joe Bennett and the
7 Cliff Bennett and the
8 Brenda and the
9 Alvin Cash and the
10 Commander Cody and his
11 Izhar Cohen and the
12 Adge Cutler and the
13 Dante and the
14 Joey Dee and the
15 Disco Tex and the
16 Julie Driscoll, Brian Auger and the
17 Eddie and the
18 Shane Fenton and the
19 Goldie and the

20 Jimmy James and the
21 Jay and the
22 Johnny and the
23 Johnny Johnson and the
24 Patti LaBelle and the
25 Ronnie Lane and the
26 Gary Lewis and the
27 Huey Lewis and the
28 Limmie and the
29 Laurie Lingo and the
30 Little Anthony and the
31 Malcolm McLaren and the
32 Manuel and his
33 Sergio Mendes and
34 Garnett Mimms and the
35 Bobby "Boris" Pickett and the
36 ? and the
37 Paul Revere and the
38 Ruby and the
39 Mitch Ryder and the
40 Sam the Sham and the
41 Sheila and
42 Shep and the
43 Tony Sheridan and the
44 Shirley and
45 Spanky and
46 Gene Vincent and his
47 Johnny Wakelin and the
48 Geno Washington and the
49 Maurice Williams and the
50 Young Steve and the

 C

1 Laurel Aitken and the
2 Lee Andrews and the
3 Bobby Angelo and the
4 Freddie Bell and the
5 Jet Bronx and the
6 Linda Carr and the
7 Cat Mother and the

47 Peter Straker and the

48 Sunny and the

49 Billy Ward and the

50 J Frank Wilson and the

<table>
<tr><td>QUIZ 35</td><td>

WHAT HAVE THEY DONE TO MY SONG MA
</td></tr>
</table>

The two artists listed in the questions have both recorded versions of the same song. Name the song and the original artist in each case.

 **A**

1   Dave Edmunds, Ramones
2   Who, Flying Lizards
3   Bill Black's Combo, Billy Swan
4   Love Affair, Rex Smith and Rachel Sweet
5   Jerry Lee Lewis, Swinging Blue Jeans
6   Telly Savalas, Hall and Oates
7   Stranglers, Average White Band
8   Billy Fury, Child
9   Bubblerock, Devo
10 Bay City Rollers, Tourists
11 Carly Simon and James Taylor, Belle Stars
12 Sex Pistols, Telex
13 Santana, UK Subs
14 Jimmy James and the Vagabonds, UB40
15 Weathermen, KC and the Sunshine Band

 **B**

1   Pat Boone, Four Seasons
2   Johnny Kidd and the Pirates, Dave Clark Five
3   Anthony Newley, Donny Osmond
4   Linda Ronstadt, Colin Blunstone
5   Tiny Tim, Dolly Parton
6   Eric Clapton, Light Of The World
7   David Bowie, Amii Stewart
8   Lonnie Mack, Silicon Teens
9   Animals, Eddie Floyd

10　Jermaine Jackson, Cliff Richard
11　Everly Brothers, Altar Boys
12　Bill Haley and his Comets, Elvis Presley
13　Shadows, Jorgan Ingmann
14　Dave Clark Five, Child
15　Randy Crawford, Diana Ross

 **C**

1　Alan Price Set, Nina Simone
2　Cliff Richard, Donny Osmond
3　Tab Hunter, Donny Osmond
4　Jimi Hendrix, XTC
5　George Benson, Central Line
6　Tremeloes, Band
7　Jose Feliciano, Amii Stewart
8　Applejacks, Pretenders
9　Teenbeats, Dr Mix and the Remix
10　Jay and the Americans, Don McLean
11　Judge Dread, Vicious Pink Phenomena
12　Rolling Stones, Clive Langer
13　Flying Picketts, Rita Coolidge
14　Dave Stewart and Barbara Gaskin, Bryan Ferry
15　Grace Jones, Human League

Top line left to right:
1   He had 11 hits from 1956–60 and committed suicide in 1963
2   18 hits for this ex-Leeds factory worker
3   One hit in 1956 and one in 1963 for the man in the tablecloth

Right: 4   He topped the chart in 1957 as Donny Osmond did in 1973 with the same song

Far Right: 5   To him Sarah Vaughan was a passing stranger

Right: 6   He topped the charts twice in the early 50s. His daughter was the princess in *Star Wars*

Far right: 7   Nineteen hits including two number ones, featured in *The Guinness Book of British Hit Singles* but sadly died a while back in Australia

8   Filmwise a duo,
    but musically only
    one of them
    charted records

Right: 9   He charted
    for Liverpool
    before Billy Fury
    or the Beatles

Far right:
    10   Rifleman
    Williams the rock
    'n' roll star who
    turned evangelist

<table>
<tr><td>QUIZ 37</td><td>KING CREOLE</td></tr>
</table>

A brief quiz for Elvis film buffs. The answers to all these questions are the names of Elvis movies.

 **A**

1 Which was the only Elvis movie whose title song reached number one in Britain?

2 Which Elvis movie was based on a Harold Robbins book? (An extra point for correctly naming the book)

3 Which was Presley's first post-Army movie?

4 Which one was it that featured 'Can't Help Falling In Love'?

5 In one film Elvis played two parts, one in a blond wig. Name the film.

6 Which film co-starred Nancy Sinatra?

7 And which one co-starred the person who almost became Nancy Sinatra's stepmother?

8 Which was his biggest world wide box office success?

9 Which one was originally called *The Reno Brothers*?

10 Which was his first documentary feature film?

 **B**

1 Walter Matthau played the villain in one film. Which one?

2 Which one featured Charles Bronson?

3 Which film had the same title as the flipside of Alan Price's biggest hit?

4 A girl who had a number one hit of her own in the States starred in three Elvis movies. Who was she, what was the name of her number one hit, and which was the first film she starred in?

5 Which film featured Rudy Vallee?

6 Which was the first (of many) directed by Norman Taurog?

7 Which was the other one directed by the man who had directed *Jailhouse Rock*? And who was the director?

8 Which film co-starred Mary Tyler Moore as a nun?

9 Which film was produced by the producer of *Rebel Without A Cause*?

10 Which film featured 'One Broken Heart For Sale'?

 **C**

1 Which Elvis movie was a remake of a 1937 film which had been directed by the man who directed *King Creole*?

2 Which one was scripted by the man who two years later won an Oscar for his screenplay of *Becket*?

3 Which one features (very briefly) Raquel Welch taking a shower?

4 Production on which film was delayed because Elvis inhaled the crown of one of his front teeth during filming?

5 Which was Elvis' favourite of all the films he made?

6 An actress who had already had her own Top 20 hit in America co-starred in one Elvis movie, and later also co-starred with Art Garfunkel in one of his films. Who was the actress, what was the Elvis film in which she co-starred, and what was the film she made with Art Garfunkel?

7 Which film was reviewed by the *New York Times* as "the silliest, feeblest and dullest vehicle for the Memphis wonder in a long time"?

8 Which one earned this review from the *New York Times* (which clearly did not think too highly of Elvis' celluloid efforts): "Even compared to some previous Presley turkeys, this one sheds feathers from the start."?

9 Which film features a Bob Dylan track on the soundtrack album, but not in the film itself?

10 Which film earned Elvis the review, "This boy can act"?

QUIZ 38	WHAT'D I SAY

The following are spoken introductions or musical prologues to hit records. You need only identify the song. Anyone who gets them all correct should consider a career in public speaking.

 **A**

1 "Hey you! Don't watch that, watch this! This is the heavy, heavy monster sound!"

2 "Our life together is so precious together. We have grown, we have grown. Although our love is still special, let's take a chance and fly away somewhere alone."

3 "She packed my bags last night pre-flight, zero hour,

nine a.m., and I'm gonna be high as a kite by then."

4 "One, two, three o'clock, four o'clock rock."

5 "I look at all the lonely people. I look at all the lonely people."

6 "A long, long time ago, I can still remember how that music used to make me smile. And I knew if I had my chance that I could make those people dance, and maybe they'd be happy for awhile."

7 "Well it's a-one for the money, two for the show, three to get ready now go, cat, go . . ."

8 "Is this the real life? Is this just fantasy? Caught in a landslide, no escape from reality. Open your eyes, look up to the skies and see."

9 "The world is just a great big onion."

10 "C'mon everybody, clap your hands! Ah, you're lookin' good! I'm gonna sing my song, it won't take long, we're gonna do the twist and it goes like this . . ."

11 "Is she really going out with him?"

12 "I know when to go out. I know when to stay in, get things done."

13 "You'll never know how much I really love you. You'll never know how much I really care."

14 "Give me time to realize my crime. Let me love and steal. I have danced inside your eyes. How can I be real?"

15 "Happy Xmas Yoko. Happy Xmas John."

 **B**

1 "This following programme is dedicated to the city and people of San Francisco, who may not know it, but they are beautiful, and so is their city. This is a very personal song, so if the viewer cannot understand it, save up all your bread and fly Trans-Love Airways to San Francisco, U.S.A. It will be worth it, if not for the sake of this song, but for the sake of your own peace of mind."

2 "I was born and raised down in Alabama on a farm way back up in the woods."

3 "If you hate me after what I say . . . can't put it off any longer. Just got to tell her anyway."

4 "Laura and Tommy were lovers. He wanted to give her everything – flowers, presents, and most of all, a wedding ring."

5 "I've heard people say that too much of anything is no good for you, baby. But I don't know about that. As many times as we've loved, we've shared love and made love, it doesn't seem to me like it's enough."

6 "My tears are fallin' 'cause you've taken her all away. And though it really hurts me so, there's something that I've gotta say."

7 "It was a moonlit night in old Mexico. I walked along between some old adobe haciendas. Suddenly I heard the plaintive cry of a young Mexican girl.'

8 "To lead a better life, I need my love to be here."

9 "Here's my story, it's sad but true, 's about a girl and I once knew. She took my love then ran around with every single guy in town.'

10 "The loveliness of Paris seems somehow sadly gay. The glory that was Rome is of another day. I've been terribly alone and forgotten in Manhattan. I'm going home to my city by the bay."

11 "Soldier boy, oh my little soldier boy, I'll be true to you."

12 "She would never say where she came from. Yesterday don't matter if it's gone. While the sun is bright or in the darkest night, no one knows. She comes and goes.'

13 'If you need me, call me, no matter where you are, no matter how far. Just call my name, I'll be there in a hurry, on that you can depend and never worry. You see, my love is alive. It's like a seed that only needs the thought of you to grow. So if you feel the need for company, please my darling, let it be me."

14 "A candy-coloured clown they call The Sandman tiptoes to my room every night just to sprinkle stardust and to whisper 'Go to sleep, everything is alright.' "

15 "Once I had a pretty girl, her name it doesn't matter. She went away with another guy and now he won't even look at her."

1 "You broke my heart 'cause I couldn't dance. You didn't even want me around. And now I'm back, to let you know I can really shake 'em down."

2 "Everybody say 'yeah.' ('yeah.') Say 'yeah.' ('yeah.') Say 'yeah,' ('yeah'), 'yeah,' ('yeah'), 'yeah,' 'yeah,' 'yeah.' "

3 "I remember my first love affair. Somehow or another the whole darn thing went wrong. But my mother had some great advice so I thought I'd put it in the words of this song."

4 "Happy birthday. Happy birthday, baby. Oh, I love you so."

5 "The night was clear and the moon was yellow and the leaves came tumbling down."

6 "He gets up each morning and he goes downtown,

where everyone's his boss and he's lost in an angry land. He's a little man."

7 "I'll be alone each and every night. While you're away, don't forget to write."

8 "Does he love me? I wanna know. How can I tell if he loves me so?"

9 "The rain and thinking of you. Soon as I get home I'm gonna call you and tell you how much I love you. Oh, I feel so good.'

10 "Hello honey it's me. What did you think when you heard me back on the radio? What did the kids say when they knew it was their long lost Daddio?"

11 "These are the words of a frontier lad who lost his love when he turned bad."

12 "Hello, I'm Johnny Cash."

13 "Darling, may I have the pleasure of having this next twist with you? You don't know how to twist? Well, let me tell you!"

14 "Every time my baby and I have a quarrel, I swear I won't give in. Then my baby starts to smile at me, and I know, I know, I just can't win."

15 "People always ask me 'How do you make a hit record?' And I tell them 'It's you, the public, who make the hit records.' "

| QUIZ 39 | LOOKING AFTER NUMBER ONE |

1 What was the first number one on Mickie Most's RAK label?

2 Which of the following Birmingham groups have never had a number one as a solo act; The Moody Blues, The Move, The Electric Light Orchestra, UB40?

3 Which record is generally accepted as the first reggae chart-topper?

4 Which singer had to wait the longest time between number one hits?

5 What was number one when the *New Musical Express* published Britain's first singles chart?

6 Which Beatles' number one featured Billy Preston on keyboards?

7 Which John Lennon song did Roxy Music record as a tribute to him and went to number one in March 1981?

8 Out of Elvis Presley's 17 number ones only one had a single word title. Which one?

9 What are the real surnames of two time chart-toppers the Walker Brothers?

10 Which two painters have been the subjects of number one records?

11 Which number one was written by a Womble?

12 What was the last number one (so far) produced by George Martin?

13 Which record was number one at the end of the sixties and beginning of the seventies?

14 Which film theme was released in 1970 but didn't make number one until 1980?

15 Which group made the top with each of their first three releases?

 **B**

1 What was the Beatles' last number one on the Parlophone label?

2 What was the first UK number one for the Warner Brothers label and why was it especially pleasing for the company?

3 Chas Chandler's first taste of the number one spot was in 1964 as the Animal's bass player on 'House Of The Rising Sun'. His next was in 1971 as producer of which record and by whom?

4 What was the only Rolling Stones number one to feature Mick Taylor?

5 What was the difference between Abba's first six number ones and their last three?

6 Whose first two number ones as a solo artist both featured the word "Eyes" in their titles?

7 Which number one included the full title of the preceding chart topper in its own title?

8 Whose second number one was called 'Baby Jump'?

9 Which five non-Beatle acts have had number ones with Lennon/McCartney songs?

10 On 11 April 1963 Gerry and the Pacemakers became the first Merseybeat band to reach the chart summit. Who did they dislodge from the top spot?

11 Which member of Pink Floyd was partly responsible for Kate Bush's success and number one record 'Wuthering Heights'?

12 Who wrote 'One Day At A Time', a number one for Lena Martell?

13 Which 1969 number one was subtitled 'Exordium And Terminus'?

14 Which number one was sung by Ron Dante, Barry Manilow's co-producer?

15 Bob Dylan hasn't yet had a number one as a performer but two of his compositions have been chart-toppers. Which two?

 **C**

1 Who wrote Buddy Holly's posthumous number one 'It Doesn't Matter Anymore'?

2 When Les Reed and Gordon Mills wrote 'It's Not Unusual', a number one for Tom Jones, who did they have in mind to record it?

3 What is the connection between Hot Chocolate's number one 'So You Win Again' and Unit 4 + 2's 'Concrete And Clay'?

4 Which 1961 chart-topper was an adaption of a German folk song 'Muss I Denn'?

5 Who originally recorded 'D.I.V.O.R.C.E.' which gave Billy Connolly a number one with his parody version?

6 Which 1978 number one was said to plagiarise the song 'Taj Mahal' by Jorge Ben?

7 Terry Jacks had a 1974 number one with 'Seasons In The Sun'. Which group had he previously charted with?

8 Who produced Bill Haley and his Comets number one 'Rock Around The Clock'?

9 Soft Cell's number one 'Tainted Love' was written by Ed Cobb. Which High School band had he been a member of?

10 The Byrd's 'Mr Tambourine Man' was produced by the son of a famous actress. Who was he and who was his mother?

11 Gerry and the Pacemakers' third number one 'You'll Never Walk Alone' was taken from a film. What was the film and who performed the song in the film?

12 What was the aptly titled follow up flop to the Kalin Twin's number one?

13 Who originally recorded 'Bye Bye Baby' a number one for the Bay City Rollers?

14 Who were the first female duo to top the British charts?

15 What was the first instrumental to top the chart and what, so far, is the last?

<table>
<tr><td>QUIZ 40</td><td>I GET AROUND</td></tr>
</table>

Fill in the missing modes of transport.

1　Joe Dowell – 'Little Red Rented . . . . .'
2　Burt Bacharach – '. . . . . And . . . . . And . . . . .'
3　Mixtures – 'The . . . . . Song'
4　Hondells – 'Little . . . . .'
5　Hot Chocolate – 'Heaven's In The Back Seat Of My . . . . .'
6　Monkees – 'Last . . . . . To Clarksville'
7　Steve Miller – '. . . . .'
8　Wurzels – '. . . . .'
9　Peter Paul and Mary – 'Leaving On A . . . . .'
10　Queen – '. . . . . Race'

<table>
<tr><td>QUIZ 41</td><td>HERE THERE AND EVERYWHERE</td></tr>
</table>

The answers to all these clues are places – towns, countries, streets, continents or planets. Many are song titles, some are not.

1　Abba's number one battlefield and a railway station
2　The country that cried for Julie Covington
3　Scott McKenzie's flower city
4　The almost unspellable place the Bee Gees have been
5　A band and Frank Sinatra's kind of town
6　The ancient city by whose rivers Boney M wept
7　Where Wings' desire is always to be
8　Where the barber shaves another customer in Liverpool
9　Where the Beach Boys wish all girls could come from
10　The city whose streets were serenaded by Ralph McTell
11　Gerry Rafferty's street
12　A label, a planet and Queen's lead singer
13　Frankie Avalon's goddess, Mark Wynter's blue-jeaned girl, and a planet

14 Duran Duran's planet

15 Where Glen Campbell will be by the time she's rising

16 Pink Floyd's dark side

17 The Righteous Brothers' white cliffs

18 Hometown of Little Jimmy Osmond's long haired lover

19 The town Roger Whittaker is leaving

20 David Sylvian's band

 **B**

1 David Essex's island

2 The state on Ray Charles' mind

3 Where Bonnie Tyler was lost

4 Lonnie Donegan said it "ain't nowhere, fifteen miles from Middlesbrough"

5 Where Dionne Warwick asked the way to

6 Kim Wilde's Southeast Asian communist stronghold

7 Lou Busch and the Piranhas hit with this river

8 Johnny Duncan didn't miss this last train

9 The Monkees didn't miss this last train

10 Match for the Style Council

11 Dave Dee, Dozy, Beaky, Mick and Tich and the Electric Light Orchestra and Olivia Newton-John's paradise

12 "Long distance information, more than that I cannot add"

13 Connie Francis' moon

14 Elvis Presley's blue moon state

15 Where Jam planted an 'A' Bomb

16 Barry Manilow's triangle

17 Where Jojo left his home and should have got back to

18 Pussycat state

19 Joni Mitchell was on Max Yasgur's farm there

20 Where Simon and/or Garfunkel is the only living boy

 **C**

1 New Vaudeville Band tube station

2 Lucky Kentucky town with a bias for Don and Phil

3 Where the Grand Coulee Dam makes factories hum

4 Where the special rose has never seen the sun

5 Where Three Dog Night have never been

6 Elvis' special train

7 What did Delaware?

8 Special guns

9   Where you'll get a fair price for parsley, sage, rosemary and thyme

10 Coming in, bringing in a couple of keys

11 City train, where Fats Domino is walking

12 Say you will, Jackson Browne

13 Kraftwerk's 1983 national Tour

14 Not Frankie Vaughan's Constantinople

15 Kokomo's small continent

16 Diamond Head album city

17 Johnny Wakelin's band

18 Where the Kansas City Star's letter just this morning was postmarked

19 The destination of the third boxcar, midnight train

20 Where I woke up high over, on my way to the Promised Land

| QUIZ 42 | I'M GONNA SIT RIGHT DOWN AND WRITE MYSELF A LETTER |

This is another word puzzle. Complete it in the same way as the one at Quiz 18.

A   Artists who performed the lyric you are looking for (4,5)
    PAUL SIMON and (3,9)
    ART GARFUNKEL

B   Album in which this lyric appeared (8)
    BOOKENDS

C   Hit single by Rock Follies stars Julie Covington, Rula Lenska, Charlotte Cornwell and Sue Jones-Davies (2)
    _OK_

D   They changed their name from Chicago Transit Authority (7) _CHICAGO_

E   1970 number one, '_BRIDGE OVER_ Troubled _WATER_' (6,4,5)

F   '_I SEE_ The Moon,' Stargazers' number one (1,3)

G   Ray Stevens' Bridget was one (6) _MIDGET_

H   They got on the cover of Rolling Stone by singing about it (2,4) _DR HOOK_

I   Paul McCartney and Michael Jackson's second hit duet, '_SAY SAY_ Say' (3,3)

J   One of Abba's three 1976 number ones (5,3)
    MAMMA MIA

K   According to Gary Numan, what happens when you die? (1,3) _I DIE_

L Second UK hit single by artists who recorded the quotation (1,2,1,4) I AM A ROCK

M Jeff Beck's singalong standard, 'HI Ho Silver Lining' (2)

N What happens when Dave Edmunds and the Stray Cats sing a George Jones song (3,4,2,2)
THE RACE IS ON

O The only kind of polka Brian Hyland ever sang (3)
DOT

P First word of title of Badfinger song covered by Nilsson (7)
WITHOUT

Q Herb named in title of album by artists who recorded quotation (5) THYME

R Robert Wyatt's Machine (4) SOFT

S Relation to writer of quotation of daughter of American vocalist with two 1953 number ones (4) WIFE

T Where Phil Spector played a guitar solo for the Drifters:
ON Broadway (2)

THE SHOW MUST GO ON

These questions are all related to records that are in some way connected with the theatre and cinema.

From what show did the following songs come from and who had the biggest UK hit record with each song?

A

1 'Memory'
2 'On The Street Where You Live'
3 'I'd Be Surprisingly Good For You'
4 'Somewhere'
5 'Send In The Clowns'
6 'Hernando's Hideaway'
7 'Good Morning Starshine'
8 'As Long As He Needs Me'
9 'Day By Day'
10 'Spread A Little Happiness'
11 'No Other Love'
12 'People'
13 'Happy Talk'
14 'Stranger In Paradise'
15 'Genie With The Light Brown Lamp'

And now the movie that first gave us these songs, and the act that had the biggest UK hit with same:

B

1 'You're The One That I Want'
2 'Out Here On My Own'
3 'The Morning After'
4 'When The Girl In Your Arms Is The Girl In Your Heart'
5 'Rock-A-Hula-Baby'
6 'The Rose'
7 'Eye Of The Tiger'
8 'Nobody Does It Better'
9 'Silver Dream Machine'
10 'Call Me'
11 'Evergreen'
12 'How Deep Is Your Love'

13   'All Time High'

14   'You Light Up My Life'

15   'Three Coins In The Fountain'

 C

1   Which film soundtrack album was the biggest selling LP of all time before it was overtaken by Thriller?

2   What was the title of the movie that starred Abba?

3   Which Presley films introduced (a) 'Hard Headed Woman' (b) 'Can't Help Falling In Love' (c) '(Let Me Be Your) Teddy Bear' (d) 'Bossa Nova Baby'?

4   Who composed and recorded the 'Theme From Shaft'?

5   She had a number two hit album in the UK in 1980 with a "concept" album which later became one half of a West End show in which she starred. (a) Who is she? (b) What was the title of the album? (c) What was the title of the hit single from the album? (d) What was the title of the West End Show?

6   What track was used in the soundtrack of the film The Exorcist although it was not written by the composer for the film? Who was the composer?

7   What was the title of the film in which Billy Fury sang 'Once Upon A Dream'?

8   Which Broadway show provided Top Five US hits for Three Dog Night and the Cowsills?

9   Which Broadway show provided Top 20 US hits for Helen Reddy and Murray Head?

10   Which movie gave Eric Weissberg and Steve Mandell an international hit single and what was the title of their hit?

11   Who had a hit in 1982 in both America and Britain with a song from the Broadway musical Dreamgirls?

12   What was the name of the movie whose soundtrack provided Lee Marvin with a surprise UK number one in 1970 with 'Wand'rin' Star'?

13   Which theme tune became, in August 1953, the first instrumental ever to top the British charts, and whose hand was on the baton?

14   Which James Bond films features songs by (a) Paul McCartney (b) Marvin Hamlisch and Carole Bayer Sager (c) Lionel Bart?

15   Which film soundtrack album topped the UK album charts for every week of one calendar year, and which year was it?

QUIZ 44	SOLDIER BOY

1 Which group sang the 'Soldier's Song'?
2 In which 1971 song didn't the singer want to be a soldier, sailor, rich man, poor man, beggar man, thief, lawyer, churchman or a failure?
3 Which chart topping lady singer invited her lover to "lay down your arms and surrender to mine" in the 50's?
4 Who sang about tanks rolling over Poland?
5 Who recorded 'You Don't Have To Be In The Army To Fight In The War'?
6 What rank was Barry Sadler who sang 'The Ballad Of The Green Berets'?
7 In 1981 XTC sang of Sergeant Rock. Which two army ranks had they vocalised about the previous year?
8 First used during World War II they bounced back musically in 1956
9 Who fired 'Machine Gun Etiquette' into the album chart in 1979?
10 Which Scotsman declared 'The Battle's O'er' in 1961?

QUIZ 45	MY NAME IS JACK

This load of questions deals with the names, real and imagined, of recording acts. The answer to each is a name, or occasionally, names.

What are the first names of:

1 Simon and Garfunkel
2 Hall and Oates

What are the surnames of:

3 Cliff and Hank
4 Nancy and Lee
5 John and Yoko

Which recording act took its name from:

6   A character in the Jane Fonda film *Barbarella*
7   A clothes shop in Paris
8   The initials of their four members
9   A mixture of champagne and orange juice
10   A pun on an insect's name

By what names are these people better known?

11   Richard Starkey
12   Harry Webb
13   David Jones
14   George O'Dowd
15   Gordon Sumner
16   Marie Frieda née Lawrie
17   Arnold George Dorsey
18   Reg Dwight
19   Priscilla White
20   Charles Hardin Holley
21   Tommy Hicks
22   Gary Webb
23   Ernest Jennings Ford
24   Doris von Kappelhoff
25   Robert Zimmermann

What are the first names of:

1   Sylvian Sakamoto
2   Godley and Creme

What are the surnames of:

3   Jan and Dean
4   Peter and Gordon
5   Sonny and Cher

Which recording act took its name from:

6   A T S Eliot cat
7   A government unemployment form

8   A guitar echo device (spelt wrong)
9   The fact that they were "one over the eight"
10 Their original financial position

By what names are these people better known?:

11 Mary O'Brien
12 Thomas Woodward
13 Clive Powell
14 Terry Nelhams
15 J P Richardson
16 Michael McCartney
17 Richard Sarstedt
18 Paul Gadd
19 John Deutschendorf
20 Vincent Furnier
21 Trevor Stanford
22 Marc Feld
23 Mary Sandeman
24 Kevin Parrott and Michael Coleman
25 Wynette Pugh

What are the first names of:

1   McGuinness Flint
2   Zager and Evans

What are the surnames of:

3   Hugo and Luigi
4   Althia and Donna
5   Alfi and Harry

Which group took its name from:

6   A Western starring John Wayne?
7   A spirit at an ouija board
8   The site of an American Civil War battle
9   A film starring Dirk Bogarde and Mary Ure
10 A cold Eskimo night

By what names are the following better known?:

11 Jeffrey Calvert and Max West
12 Ronald Wycherly
13 Terence Perkins
14 James Marcus Smith
15 Ross Bagdasarian
16 Sandra Goodrich
17 Paul Pond
18 William Ashton
19 Charles Westover
20 Walden Robert Cassotto
21 David Spencer
22 Harold Jenkins
23 Frank LoVecchio
24 Dino Crocetti
25 Bernard Jewry

QUIZ 46	WORDY RAPPINGHOOD

There is a word missing in the title of each of the following singles. Supply the correct word.

1 'Tie A Yellow Ribbon Round The Old . . . . . Tree,' Dawn featuring Tony Orlando
2 '(You're) Having My . . . . .,' Paul Anka
3 'Tainted . . . . .,' Soft Cell
4 'I Want To Hold Your . . . . .,' Beatles
5 'Anarchy In The . . . . .,' Sex Pistols
6 'Walking On The . . . . .,' Police
7 'Another . . . . . In The Wall,' Pink Floyd
8 'I'm Not In . . . . .,' 10 CC
9 'When You're In Love With A Beautiful . . . . .,' Dr Hook
10 'How Much Is That . . . . . In The Window,' Lita Roza
11 'Red Red . . . . .,' UB 40
12 'Gonna Make You A . . . . .,' David Essex
13 'Don't You Want . . . . .,' Human League

14 'How Deep Is Your . . . . .,' Bee Gees

15 'Ebony And . . . . .,' Paul McCartney and Stevie Wonder

16 'Whole Lot Of . . . . . Goin' On,' Jerry Lee Lewis

17 'Stand And . . . . .,' Adam and the Ants

18 'House Of . . . . .,' Madness

19 'House Of The Rising . . . . .,' Animals

20 'I Heard It Through the . . . . .,' Marvin Gaye

 **B**

1 'Reasons To Be . . . . . Pt 3,' Ian Dury and the Blockheads

2 'At The . . . . .,' Danny and the Juniors

3 'At The . . . . .,' Simon and Garfunkel

4 'Born To . . . . .,' Bruce Springsteen

5 'Down The . . . . .,' Status Quo

6 'You . . . . . Me,' Sam Cooke

7 'Sultans Of . . . . .,' Dire Straits

8 '. . . . . The Pilot,' Joan Armatrading

9 'Positively . . . . . Street,' Bob Dylan

10 'Be My . . . . .,' Fats Domino

11 'Twenty-Four Hours From . . . . .,' Gene Pitney

12 'Ooh To Be . . . . .,' Kajagoogoo

13 'He's Got The Whole . . . . . In His Hands,' Laurie London

14 'If You Don't Know . . . . . By Now,' Harold Melvin and the Bluenotes

15 'Rock The . . . . .,' Clash

16 'Only . . . . .,' Craig Douglas

17 'Planet . . . . .,' Duran Duran

18 'Can The . . . . .,' Suzi Quatro

19 'A . . . . . To Remember,' Shalamar

20 'I Honestly Love . . . . .,' Olivia Newton-John

 **C**

1 'Hey . . . . . Man,' Stevie Wonder

2 'Beautiful . . . . .,' Neil Diamond

3 'The Day The World Turned . . . . .,' X-Ray Spex

4 'Wear My Ring Around Your . . . . .,' Elvis Presley

5 'Always . . . . .,' Gary Glitter

6 '. . . . . Came Today,' Jackson Five

7 'Shake Your . . . . .,' KC and the Sunshine Band

8 'Take Me To The . . . . .,' Talking Heads

9 'Bridge Of . . . . .,' David Whitfield

10 '. . . . . For You,' Tom Robinson
11 'Opus . . . . .,' Four Seasons
12 'When Something Is Wrong With My . . . . .,' Sam and Dave
13 'The Three . . . . .,' Compagnons de la Chanson
14 'Listen To The . . . . .,' Monkees
15 'Three Little . . . . .,' Bob Marley and the Wailers
16 'When The . . . . . Starts Shining In His Eyes,' Supremes
17 'You . . . . . Up My Life,' Debbie Boone
18 'Bang The . . . . . All Day,' Todd Rundgren
19 'Broken . . . . .,' Stargazers
20 'I'm Gonna Sit Right Down And Write Myself A . . . . .,' Billy Williams

QUIZ 47	LOOKING FOR CLUES

This is a variation on the **Three Steps To Heaven** quiz found elsewhere in this book. Instead of giving records recorded by the mystery artist or group it gives clues to their identity. Corresponding numbers in each of the first three parts are clues to the same act. If you correctly guess the identity using only the first clue then you can award yourself 3 points. If you need the second clue as well then you only get 2 points and if you need all three clues you only get 1 point. Needless to say if you cannot guess correctly after using all three clues you do not score at all and we recommend you buy the *Guinness Book of British Hit Singles* and its sister publications.

1 They had a minor hit in 1963 backing singer Tony Sheridan

2 His first British hit was a number one

3 He once sang alongside Long John Baldry in various blues groups

4 Three of this band's original members played together as Hotlegs shortly before the group was formed

5 His first chart entry was originally only on the chart for one week but it returned soon after and went to number one

6 As well as being a successful solo artist he also had many hits with his brothers

7 Junior Walker played on one of their records and later

recorded his own version of the song

8   He was the first person to make the US charts with a Lennon/McCartney song

9   He had a 1971 hit duetting with Georgie Fame

10   Their lead vocalist used to sing with Cyril Davis

11   They've had over ten hits without ever making the Top Ten

12   He first found chart success with the Move

13   He has had over thirty British hits without ever having a number one as a solo artist

14   They performed the soundtrack to the film *Percy*

15   He had a number one with a group of Scottish teeny-boppers

16   Their biggest hit was written by David Bowie

17   His second UK hit was also recorded by Alice Cooper

18   He is better known as a bass player and vocalist with a rock band rather than a solo artist

19   'Schoolboy Crush' was originally to have been the A-Side to his first single

20   They changed the spelling of their name after their first two hits

B

1   They split in 1970 and each member found success as a solo artist

2   He returned to his Welsh birthplace in 1983 and performed in concert

3   He had a Top Five hit singing with the group Python Lee Jackson

4   Jonathan King signed them to his UK label

5   One of his smaller UK hits was called 'Twinkle Toes'

6   He took a song to number one 16 years after Tab Hunter had taken the same song there

7   Their 1981 album '4' was in the chart for over a year

8   His real name is Charles Westover

9   He was the original keyboards player with the Animals

10   Their original guitarist died in 1969 shortly after leaving the group

11   Their first album included a version of Junior Murvin's 'Police And Thieves'

12   He joined fellow Brum Jeff Lynne in a semi-classical rock group

13   He was still a young teenager when he had his first hit

14 Songs written by their lead vocalist have been recorded by the Jam, the Applejacks and the Pretenders

15 His only solo hit was with a song previously a hit for the Walker Brothers

16 Ian Hunter was their original leader and pianist

17 He is better known as a television painter than a singer

18 He recorded the current *Top Of The Pops* theme tune

19 In 1979 he had his first number one hit for 11 years

20 Their only hit in the eighties was a cover version of a Bobby Vee song

1 They had seventeen British number ones

2 'The Green Green Grass Of Home' was his second number one

3 One of his five number ones was adapted as the theme for the BBC documentary about the crew of HMS *Ark Royal*

4 They recorded a classic slow song in 1975

5 His last British number one was 'Oh Pretty Woman'

6 His little brother Jimmy also had a number one hit

7 Their only Top Ten single so far is 'Waiting For A Girl Like You'

8 'Runaway' was his first British hit

9 He had a 1967 hit with a Randy Newman song, 'Simon Smith and His Amazing Dancing Bear'

10 Their mammoth 1981 tour resulted in the live album 'Still Life'

11 They released a triple album called 'Sandinista'

12 As a soloist his biggest hit was 'Forever' in 1973

13 'Hotter Than July' is his most successful album

14 They returned to the British Top 20 in 1983 after an eleven year absence

15 His most consistent success came when he replaced John Foxx in a synthesiser based band

16 'Roll Away The Stone' was their last top ten hit

17 He had the last number one of the sixties

18 His first hit with his group was with an old Irish folk song, 'Whiskey In The Jar'

19 The Shadows were his backing group for many years

20 Their lead vocalist had a hit duetting with Suzi Quatro

<table>
<tr><td>QUIZ 48</td><td> OH WHAT A CIRCUS</td></tr>
</table>

QUIZ 48	OH WHAT A CIRCUS

1 Which musical did the title of this quiz come from?
2 Whose clown died in 1967?
3 Who balanced on the highwire in 1975?
4 A group who emerged in 1983 and sound like a solo balancing act
5 An American label under which most circuses are performed
6 Whose circus is performing on Saturday at Bishopsgate?
7 In the song referred to in number 6 above, who danced the waltz?
8 Who invited you to step right in and see the main attraction?
9 Which famous drummer starred in *Circus Boy* when he was a lad?
10 Who sang "I want to be your acrobat" and in which song?

QUIZ 49	FIRST CUT IS THE DEEPEST

This section is easy if you have the *Guinness Book Of British Hit Singles* by your side, but a lot more difficult if you haven't. May we suggest you burn your copy before attempting these questions, and then buy a new copy after you have finished.

All we are asking is what was the title of the first British hit single for the artists named below and secondly, who performed the songs listed below, which each gave the artist in question his or her first British hit.

What was the first British hit for:

1 The Beatles
2 Tom Jones
3 Abba
4 The Shadows

5   Duran Duran
6   Billy J Kramer and the Dakotas
7   Queen
8   Paul McCartney
9   Adam and the Ants
10 Bad Manners
11 Buck's Fizz
12 Culture Club
13 Mungo Jerry
14 Julio Iglesias
15 P P Arnold
16 The Moody Blues
17 Gary Numan/Tubeway Army
18 The Wombles
19 The Righteous Brothers
20 The Four Seasons

Whose first single hit in Britain was:

21 'Heartbreak Hotel'
22 'Space Oddity'
23 'Tainted Love'
24 'Your Song'
25 'Anarchy In The UK'
26 'Only The Lonely'
27 'Move It'
28 'Virginia Plain'
29 'American Pie'
30 'The Prince'
31 'Denis'
32 'Watching The Detectives'
33 'Sylvia's Mother'
34 'Who's Sorry Now'
35 'Release Me'
36 'In The City'
37 'Everyone's Gone To The Moon'
38 'A Little Peace'
39 'Love To Love You Baby'
40 'Can't Stand Losing You'

What was the first British hit single for:

 **B**

1 The Animals
2 Cilla Black
3 Bob Marley
4 Hot Chocolate
5 The Beach Boys
6 KC and the Sunshine Band
7 Electric Light Orchestra
8 Leo Sayer
9 Chuck Berry
10 Olivia Newton-John
11 Altered Images
12 The Bachelors
13 The Bee Gees
14 Elkie Brooks
15 Dave Clark Five
16 Joe Cocker
17 Bob Dylan
18 David Essex
19 Buddy Holly
20 Human League

Whose first hit single in Britain was:

21 'Come On'
22 'Tom Dooley'
23 'Hey Rock and Roll'
24 'Don't Treat Me Like A Child'
25 'Stop Your Sobbing'
26 'Please Don't Touch'
27 'Everybody Salsa'
28 'Reach Out And Touch'
29 'Hold Me'
30 'Pictures Of Matchstick Men'
31 'Keep On Dancing'
32 'Daddy Cool'
33 'Daddy Cool – The Girl Can't Help it'
34 'Darktown Strutter's Ball'

35 'Hot Dog'
36 'I'm A Man'
37 'You Send Me'
38 'Wrapping Paper'
39 'You Make It Move'
40 'Black Magic Woman'

What was the first British hit single for:

1   Shirley Bassey
2   Led Zeppelin
3   Simon and Garfunkel
4   Frank Sinatra
5   Squeeze
6   Barbra Streisand
7   Chris Farlowe
8   The Jacksons
9   Bryan Ferry
10 Frank Ifield
11 George Benson
12 Glen Campbell
13 Ray Charles
14 Desmond Dekker and the Aces
15 Dollar
16 Marvin Gaye
17 Genesis
18 The Hollies
19 Japan
20 Johnny Mathis

Whose first British hit single was:

21 'Summer Set'
22 'United We Stand'
23 'The Little Shoemaker'
24 'Rebel Rouser'
25 'Maybe Tomorrow'
26 'Crazy'
27 'Hold Me Tight'
28 'Mary's Boy Child'

29 'Life Begins At The Hop'
30 'Good Morning Little Schoolgirl'
31 'Searchin''
32 'Shake Rattle And Roll'
33 'Dance Stance'
34 'Running Free'
35 'I'm In Love Again'
36 'Lonely Teenager'
37 'Rama Lama Ding Dong'
38 'Istanbul'
39 'Faith Can Move Mountains'
40 'Saturday Nite'

QUIZ 50	DETROIT CITY

The following questions all relate to the Tamla Motown family of artists. A knowledgeable pop fan should get Group A right. A Motown fan should find Group B bearable. If you breeze through Group C, you are a Motown employee.

1   Who wrote both 'My Guy' and 'My Girl'?
2   What female Motown artist successfully covered Harold Melvin and the Bluenotes' 'Don't Leave Me This Way'?
3   Gary Byrd co-wrote 'The Crown' with whom?
4   The first release on the Riva label was a hit re-make of an Isley Brothers smash. Who was the artist and what was the song?
5   Whose birthday was Stevie Wonder celebrating on 'Happy Birthday'?
6   What instrument did Junior Walker play?
7   Which Motown artist co-wrote 'Wherever I Lay My Hat'?
8   Who had a Northern Soul smash with 'There's A Ghost In My House'?
9   The Carpenters reached number two with a re-make of what Tamla hit?
10 What was Diana Ross' 1971 number one?
11 Marvin Gaye had a Top Ten hit with a song taken to the US Top Ten by Dion. What was it?
12 What Jimmy Ruffin track was a Top Ten hit twice?

13 What was Marvin Gaye and Tammi Terrell's biggest hit?

14 A group of Rick James proteges reached the Top 20 in 1983. Who were they and what was their hit?

15 What was the name of Jimmy Ruffin's brother and what group did he sing with?

16 To what Motown artist was Stevie Wonder once married?

17 What was Smokey Robinson's solo number one?

18 Which Jackson Five hit proved a bigger success for Gloria Gaynor?

19 Who was the lead singer of the Four Tops?

20 His biggest pre-Tamla Motown hit was 'Stop Her On Sight (SOS).' His biggest hit afterwards was 'Contact.' What was his most successful Tamla Motown release?

21 What was Lionel Richie's first solo hit?

22 With whom did Syreeta duet on 'With You I'm Born Again'?

23 What was Michael Jackson's number one on Motown?

24 The Miracles had a Top Three hit without Smokey Robinson. What was it?

25 Which Commodores hit was an instrumental?

 B

1 Who first recorded 'Ain't No Mountain High Enough'?

2 What was the Supremes' first hit without Diana Ross?

3 On what album did 'Inner City Blues (Make Me Wanna Holler)' appear?

4 The Flying Lizards had a re-make smash with what Tamla song by which Tamla artist?

5 Who originally recorded the song that gave the Supremes and Four Tops a Top 20 duet?

6 Which Motown artist was, at least through the end of 1983, a one-hit wonder . . . one number one and no other chart record?

7 'Love Child' by Diana Ross and the Supremes had a follow-up with a similarly scandalous subject matter. What was it?

8 What group had hit re-makes in the States with the Temptations' 'Get Ready' and '(I Know) I'm Losing You'?

9 The Marvelettes scored with a song that had a telephone number as its title. What was it?

10 Who were originally known as The Primes?

11 Who was Diana Ross' replacement as lead singer of the Supremes?

12 What was Michael Jackson's first solo hit?

13 The Miracles recorded Tamla's first million-seller. What was it?

14 On which Stevie Wonder classic did Jim Gilstrap of 'Swing Your Daddy' fame actually sing the first two lines?

15 Gladys Knight and the Pips' biggest UK hit on Tamla Motown as 'Help Me Make It Through the Night.' Who wrote it?

16 Holland-Dozier-Holland were the most famous Motown writing and production team. What were their Christian names?

17 'Just My Imagination (Running Away With Me)' had the longest chart run of any Temptations single, but which of their hits got higher in the Top Ten?

18 Which Stevie Wonder album included 'Superstition'?

19 In which Tamla number one did Pagliacci get a name check?

20 Which Motown artist co-wrote 'Dancing In The Street'?

21 Which popular English songstress recorded an album for Tamla Motown called 'Great Expectations'?

22 Anthony Perkins starred in which Motown movie?

23 What was the follow-up to 'Reach Out I'll Be There'?

24 Blood Sweat and Tears charted with a song originally recorded by which Motown artist?

25 Claudette Rodgers was an original member of what group?

 C

1 On which Foreigner single did Junior Walker appear?

2 On what Tamla hit did an American Indian chant?

3 What Mary Wells track was about schizophrenia?

4 The Undisputed Truth's big US hit was 'Smiling Faces Sometimes.' Their only British chart hit, however, was a different record on a different label. What was it?

5 'Keep On Truckin' was one of Eddie Kendricks' two solo hits. What was the other?

6 What was the first number one on the Tamla Motown label?

7 On which Tamla Motown hit were police sirens heard?

8 The Beatles recorded which Miracles song?

9 What was Marvin Gaye's first UK chart record?

10 What Motown artist was known as 'Obie'?

11 On what US label did Berry Gordy release Martin Luther

King's 'I Have A Dream' speech as a single?

12 Marvin Gaye wrote the soundtrack to what film?

13 Who had the biggest hit on the Mowest label?

14 The Temptations' highest charting album included 'You're My Everything,' 'All I Need,' and '(I Know) I'm Losing You.' What was it?

15 Whose unusual single combined 'What The World Needs Now Is Love' and 'Abraham, Martin And John' with interview material?

16 Motorhead made the Top Ten with a cover of 'Leaving Here.' Which Motown artist originated the number?

17 Dennis Edwards replaced David Ruffin in the Temptations. In what well-known group had he previously sung?

18 What was Marvin Gaye and Mary Wells' chart tune?

19 What Four Tops album had the longest run in the LP chart?

20 What Tamla Motown artist wrote and originally recorded 'Devil With A Blue Dress,' a US smash for Mitch Ryder?

21 Of which group was Edward Patten a member?

22 Holland-Dozier-Holland co-wrote one song with Frank DeVol. What was it?

23 The Velvelettes' popular singles 'He Was Really Saying Something' and 'Needle in a Haystack' never actually charted. What was their hit?

24 On what Stevie Wonder single did the Jackson Five appear?

25 Berry Gordy began his boxing career in what weight division?

<table>
<tr><td>QUIZ 51</td><td># LABELLED WITH LOVE</td></tr>
</table>

This section is devoted to that part of a record that never gets played – the bit in the middle, the label. Some labels, notably Tamla Motown and London-American at their peak, have inspired almost as much consumer devotion as any artist. So here are some questions for those who look lovingly at their discs as often as they listen to them.

Which UK labels provided at least one hit for each of the following acts?

1 Beatles, Adam Faith, Wings
2 Roy Orbison, Bobby Vee, Little Richard
3 Michael Jackson, Stevie Wonder, Supremes
4 Michael Jackson, Abba, Barbara Dickson
5 M, Musical Youth, Barbara Dickson
6 Billy Joel, Johnny Mathis, Earth Wind and Fire
7 Kajagoogoo, Cliff Richard, Iron Maiden
8 Elkie Brooks, Joe Jackson, Herb Alpert
9 David Bowie, Eurythmics, Hall and Oates
10 David Essex, Boomtown Rats, Tears For Fears
11 Culture Club, Human League, China Crisis
12 Manfred Mann, Louis Armstrong, Elvis Presley
13 Vera Lynn, Tommy Steele, Tom Jones
14 Procol Harum, Move, Joy Strings
15 Elton John, Jasper Carrott, Mr Bloe

In each of the following groups of four acts, three have had at least one UK hit on the same label. Which is the odd act out and what is the label common to the other three?

1 Lulu, Nashville Teens, Engelbert Humperdinck, Love Affair
2 Lulu, Neil Sedaka, Sweet, Slade
3 Lulu, Cilla Black, Nina and Frederick, Peter and Gordon
4 Lulu, Hollies, Shadows, Everly Brothers
5 Lulu, Julie Covington, Elaine Paige, Marti Webb
6 Lulu, Jim Gilstrap, Chelsea F.C., William Devaughn
7 Tracey Ullman, Bad Manners, Belle Stars, Madness

8 O'Jays, Billy Paul, Barry White, Three Degrees

9 Bananarama, Blondie, Jethro Tull, Fun Boy Three

10 Mud, Hot Chocolate, Suzi Quatro, Sweet

11 B. A. Robertson, B. A. Robertson and Maggie Bell, Maggie Bell, Dave Edmunds

12 Bob Marley and The Wailers, Pioneers, Bad Company, U2

13 Brian Poole and The Tremeloes, Tremeloes, Bob Dylan, Andy Williams

14 Genesis, Phil Collins, Clifford T. Ward, Gary Shearston

15 Kids From Fame, Joy Division, Bonnie Tyler, Kenny Everett

C

1 What do the initials A & M stand for?

2 Only one UK label has had 50 number one hits. Which?

3 Which UK recording act has had hits on six different labels?

4 Which UK number one hit changed labels in the middle of its (first) chart run?

5 Who are the leading lights of the Korova label?

6 Why do Tamla Motown records in the UK have the prefix TMG before the record number?

7 Which group scored the only number one hit single for the budget LP label Music For Pleasure?

8 Who have hit with Polydor, Brunswick, Track and Reaction in the UK?

9 Which American label, launched in Britain in 1960, scored what is still its greatest UK success with its first release, and with what record?

10 Which two UK chart labels were founded by Larry Page?

11 Name the independent label owned and created by Joe Meek, producer extraordinaire, which produced only one top ten hit during its short life.

12 Name the labels formed by (a) The Beach Boys, (b) Led Zeppelin, (c) Rod Stewart, (d) Frank Sinatra, (e) Elton John

13 A Flock Of Seagulls have had hits on the Jive label, which was not the label of one-hit wonders Typically Tropical. What's the connection?

14 Which is the odd label out and why: Red Bird, Kama Sutra, Charly, Contempo, Philadelphia International?

15 Which group leader of the 60s had two top ten hits and eight other hits on a label that shared his name?

QUIZ 52	THE ZOO

1 Who recorded 'At The Zoo'?
2 Which animal rests in the Boomtown Rats' graveyard?
3 What state was Russ Conway's penguin in?
4 Who took the paws of a big cat to number one?
5 'Apricot Brandy' was the theme to the Old Radio One programme *What's New*. Which group performed it?
6 Elton's 1972 rock
7 They evolved from Mott the Hoople
8 Which legendary British over-the-top funsters referred to "the sweet essence of giraffe" in one of their songs?
9 Who sang about a platypus duck and a wallaby in his antipodean anthem?
10 The Beatles wrote about this animal whilst sitting with Donovan in India on a visit to the Maharishi

QUIZ 53	WHO CAN IT BE NOW?

In this section we list the members of different groups/bands, and all you have to do is give the name of the group.

1 John Lennon, Paul McCartney, George Harrison, Ringo Starr
2 "Marco, Merrick, Terry Lee, Gary Tibbs and yours truly"
3 Mick Jagger, Keith Richard, Brian Jones, Charlie Watts, Bill Wyman
4 Diana Ross, Mary Wilson, Florence Ballard
5 Hank B Marvin, Bruce Welch, Jet Harris, Tony Meehan
6 David Jones, Peter Tork, Mike Nesmith, Micky Dolenz
7 Alan Price, Eric Burdon, Chas Chandler, John Steel, Hylton Valentine
8 Ray Davies, Dave Davies, Pete Quaife, Mick Avory
9 Bobby Elliott, Tony Hicks, Allan Clarke, Graham Nash, Eric Haydock
10 Tony Orlando, Joyce Vincent, Thelma Hopkins

11 Buddy Holly, Jerry Allison, Joe B Mauldin

12 Mike Pender, John McNally, Tony Jackson, Chris Curtis

13 Scott Engel, John Maus, Gary Leeds

14 Peter Green, Mick Fleetwood, John McVie, Jeremy Spencer, Danny Kirwan

15 Gerry Marsden, Fred Marsden, Les Chadwick, Les Maguire

 **B**

1 Jim Morrison, Robbie Krieger, Ray Manzarek, John Densmore

2 Jaime Robbie Robertson, Rick Danko, Richard Manuel, Garth Hudson, Levon Helm

3 Dave Stewart, Annie Lennox

4 John Sebastian, Zal Yanovsky, Steve Boone, Joe Butler

5 Arthur Lee, John Echols, Bryan Maclean, Ken Forssi, Michael Stuart

6 Alan Paul, Janis Siegel, Laurel Masse, Tim Hauser

7 Marc Almond, Dave Ball

8 Billy Davis Jr, Marilyn McCoo, Florence La Rue Gordon, Ron Townson, Lamont McLemore

9 Glenn Tilbrook, John Bentley, Jools Holland, Chris Difford, Gilson Lavis

10 Chuck Negron, Cory Wells, Danny Hutton

11 Roger McGough, John Gorman, Mike McGear

12 Stuart Elliott, Jim Cregan, Duncan Mackay, George Ford

13 Tom Scholz, Brad Delp, Barry Goudreau, Sib Hashian, Fran Sheehan

14 Randy Brecker, Dick Halligan, Jerry Weiss, Bobby Colomby, Jim Fielder, Steve Katz, Fred Lipsius, Al Kooper

15 Levi Stubbs, Renaldo Benson, Abdul Fakir, Lawrence Payton

 **C**

1 Pete Thomas, Bruce Thomas, Steve Neive

2 Peter Noone, Derek Leckenby, Keith Hopwood, Barry Whitwarn, Karl Green

3 Shirley Alston, Doris Jackson, Micky Harris, Beverley Lee

4 Andy Newman, Speedy Keen, Jimmy McCullouch

5 George Young, Gordon Fleet, Dick Diamonde, Harry Vanda, Stevie Wright

6 Aaron Love, Russell Thompkins Jr, James Smith, Herbie Murrell, James Dunn

7 David Hungate, Bobby Kimball, Steve Lukather, David Paich, Jeff Porcaro, Steve Porcaro

8 Neil Young, Stephen Stills, Richie Furay, Jim Messina

9 George Williams, Albert C Berry III, Charles Nixon, Norman Burnett, Donald Banks

10 Rick West, Alan Blakely, Dave Munden, Chip Hawkes

11 Ray Ennis, Ralph Ellis, Les Braid, Norman Kuhlke

12 Oliver Bendt, Alicia Bendt, Dorothy Hellings, Wendy Doorsen, Mario Slijngaard

13 Ray Sawyer, Dennis LoCorriere, Rik Elswit, John Wolters, Billy Francis, Jance Garfat

14 Malcolm Allured, Dave Bartram, Romeo Challenger, Rod Deas, Russ Fields, Billy Gask, Al James, Trevor Oakes

15 Chris Amoo, Eddie Amoo, Dave Smith, Ray Lake

1 A trio of vocalists together on 'Ready Steady Go'. Who are they?

   Below:

2 What is special about this street?

3 Where is this and what is its significance?

4 The Rutles, who parodied the Beatles both on television and on record. What were their adopted names for the roles they played?

5 How many times have this trio topped the charts between them?

6 Who was the 'Hound Dog Man'?

7 He's great to pull along in the winter

8 He had a number
   two hit in the
   Spring of 1977

9 Who is this 60s
   mod girl enjoying
   her supper?

10 Who is the chap
   on the left trying
   to practise his
   ventriloquism
   with an African
   dummy?

WHO'S GONNA ROCK YOU

The following musicians have all appeared in the British charts. All you have to do is to name the instrument they played on their hit recordings. In the case of keyboard players, please specify if they are exclusively known for their piano, organ or synthesiser work. Otherwise just give their instrument as 'keyboards'.

We should mention for the benefit of aggrieved or embarrassed musicians that they have been placed in these categories not on the basis of their prowess but on the likelihood they will be identified by the reader.

 **A**

1	Eric Clapton	28	Acker Bilk
2	Elton John	29	Marvin Hamlisch
3	Mark Knopfler	30	John Moss
4	Ringo Starr	31	Hank B Marvin
5	Russ Conway	32	Stewart Copeland
6	John Taylor	33	Suzi Quatro
7	Brian May	34	Carl Palmer
8	Bo Diddley	35	Stan Getz
9	Benny Goodman	36	Cozy Powell
10	Jeff Beck	37	Vangelis
11	Carlos Santana	38	Duane Eddy
12	Herb Alpert	39	Jerry Lee Lewis
13	Bill Wyman	40	Andy Mackay
14	Rick Wakeman	41	Jimmy Page
15	Louis Armstrong	42	Fats Domino
16	James Burton	43	David Byrne
17	Tony Banks	44	Jose Feliciano
18	Ginger Baker	45	Little Richard
19	Count Basie	46	James Galway
20	George Benson	47	David Gilmour
21	Chuck Berry	48	Peter Green
22	Brian Setzer	49	Charlie Watts
23	Giorgio Moroder	50	B B King
24	Glenn Miller	51	Sammy Hagar
25	Ray Charles	52	Mick Karn
26	John McVie	53	Jimi Hendrix
27	Billy Joel	54	Steve Hackett

55	Miles Davis	58	John Bonham
56	Steve Howe	59	Stanley Clarke
57	John Lodge	60	Phil Manzanera

 **B**

1	Ferrante and Teicher	31	Andy Fletcher
2	Jean-Jacques Burnel	32	Jet Harris
3	Terry Lee Miall	33	Burundi Black
4	Richard Clayderman	34	Steve Forbert
5	Glen Campbell	35	Eddie Calvert
6	Donald Byrd	36	Deke Leonard
7	Kevin Godley	37	Mary O'Hara
8	Mason Williams	38	Roy Buchanan
9	Sly Stone	39	Kenny Ball
10	Bobby Crush	40	Robin Trower
11	Chet Atkins	41	Grover Washington, Jr
12	Mrs Mills	42	Glen Matlock
13	Johnny Dankworth	43	Winifred Atwell
14	Joe Brown	44	Mick Ronson
15	Zoot Money	45	Charlie Rich
16	Chris Barber	46	Martin Chambers
17	Tony Meehan	47	Rodney Franklin
18	Junior Walker	48	Ronnie Lane
19	David Ball	49	Ike Turner
20	George Formby	50	John du Prez
21	John Keeble	51	Tomita
22	Bill Black	52	Manitas de Playa
23	Jack Bruce	53	Patrick Moraz
24	Graham Bond	54	Jerry Allison
25	Georghe Zamfir	55	Delbert McClinton
26	J J Cale	56	Gary Moore
27	Simon Crowe	57	Dudley Moore
28	Floyd Cramer	58	Charlie Byrd
29	Humphrey Lyttleton	59	Ronnie Laws
30	Charlie Kunz		

 C

1	Rudy Pompilli	31	Kevin Peek
2	Phil Upchurch	32	Daryl Dragon
3	Jackie McLean	33	Bill Ward
4	Dick Hyman	34	Roger Williams
5	Charlie Foxx	35	Adrian Brett
6	Eric Weissberg	36	Bill Payne
7	Joe "Fingers" Carr	37	Lee Jackson
8	Elvin Bishop	38	Ed Cassidy
9	Charles Earland	39	Randy Bachman
10	Boris Gardner	40	Larry Graham
11	Raphael Ravenscroft	41	Muff Winwood
12	Norman Kuhlke	42	John Stewart
13	Mike Cotton	43	Tim Renwick
14	Lonnie Mack	44	Dee Murray
15	Johnny Pearson	45	Mick Tucker
16	Jimmy Smith	46	Andy Newman
17	Terry Lightfoot	47	Larry Carlton
18	Tony Rallo	48	Dougie Thomson
19	Gino Soccio	49	Dave Lambert
20	Tony Crombie	50	Dave Stewart
21	Dexter Wansell	51	Paul Atkinson
22	Chris Spedding	52	Mary Tarplin
23	Cozy Cole	53	Carmine Appice
24	Klaus Wunderlich	54	Richie Furay
25	Wayne Henderson	55	Dino Danelli
26	Bernie Torme	56	Paul Thompson
27	Brian Smith	57	Maurice White
28	Gordon Giltrap	58	Randy Meisner
29	Woot Steinhaus	59	Joe Sample
30	Dick Taylor	60	Larry Knechtel

<table>
<tr><td>QUIZ 56</td><td># ONE NATION UNDER A GROOVE</td></tr>
</table>

This section is all about acts who are neither British nor American but have the audacity to come from somewhere else. They don't always sing in their foreign lingo, or even with a foreign accent. Some don't even sing at all. *The Times Atlas of the World* may for once be as much help to you as one of the many Guinness Music Books in your library.

What are (or were) the nationalities of the following recording acts?

1 Abba (a gentle starter but also see Group C, clever Dick)
2 Trio
3 Focus
4 James Last
5 Julio Iglesias
6 Compagnons de la Chanson
7 Air Supply
8 Manfred Mann (the man, not any of his groups)
9 Topol
10 Los Bravos
11 Yellow Magic Orchestra
12 Men At Work
13 Blue Swede
14 Johnny Hallyday
15 Vangelis

And of these slightly less familiar names:

1 Flash And The Pan
2 Easybeats
3 Massiel
4 Prince Buster
5 Sheila (of B Devotion fame)
6 Kyu Sakamoto
7 Greyhound
8 Goombay Dance Band
9 Pussycat
10 Severine
11 Titanic

12 Georghe Zamfir
13 Shocking Blue
14 Zaine Griff
15 Placido Domingo

1 Which member of Abba is not actually from the country that gave us Volvo and Bjorn Borg?

2 From what country does he/she come from?

3 Which group were the inspiration for Jonathan King's 'Lick A Smurp For Christmas'?

4 Who were the first female vocal duo to have a number one hit in the UK and indeed the first act from their country to hit the top in Britain?

5 Who is the only other act to have come from the country that gave us the duo of question 4 to have had a number one in Britain?

6 Who found that 'History Never Repeats' after a UK Top 20 hit with 'I Got You'?

7 Where did Horst Jankowski walk?

8 Which French producer/composer is married to an international film star and has had one of his chart hits taken back into the Top 50 by the Shadows?

9 And what was the name of that hit?

10 What do South African girl group Clout and the Who have in common?

11 Which of the following major personalities or acts of our time do not come from either the UK or the USA: The Bee Gees, Olivia Newton-John, Sam the Sham and the Pharaohs, Seekers, New Seekers, Paul Anka, Japan?

12 Which group of West Indian origin recorded the second biggest selling single in British record history and in which country was it recorded?

13 What do the following foreigners have in common?: Lys Assia, Jacqueline Boyer, Milk and Honey, Vicky Leandros, Anne-Marie David

14 And which is the odd one out of the five acts listed in question 13?

15 What is the lyrical connection between Charles Aznavour, Peter Sellers and Sophia Loren?

<table>
<tr><td>QUIZ 57</td><td>GARDEN OF EDEN</td></tr>
</table>

1   Who was famous for tiptoeing through the tulips?
2   Who never promised you a rose garden in 1971?
3   Who planted a 'Forget Me Not' in 1962?
4   Motorhead became Top 20 diggers with this in 1980?
5   What did the Move hear in the garden?
6   What did they sit on at our daughter's wedding?
7   Which group adopted a West Country accent when they sang 'Me I'm just a lawnmower you can tell by the way I walk'?
8   Which American 60s group were pushin' too hard?
9   Which group took their name from the inventor of the seed drill?
10 Which Tornado went on to extract vegetables from his garden?

<table>
<tr><td>QUIZ 58</td><td>STUCK IN THE MIDDLE WITH YOU</td></tr>
</table>

In each group of names listed in this section, there is one odd man out. For example, in the first group of Ringo Starr, Bill Wyman and Paul McCartney, the odd man out is Bill Wyman, who was never a Beatle. The more obscure choice of Ringo as the only drummer or Paul as the only left-hander is not permissible. We are not trying to be too clever by half.

1   Ringo Starr, Bill Wyman, Paul McCartney
2   Shane Fenton, Alvin Stardust, Billy Fury
3   Ritchie Valens, Big Bopper, Buddy Holly, Bobby Vee
4   'Jailhouse Rock', 'Heartbreak Hotel', Living Doll', 'Suspicious Minds'
5   'Kissing To Be Clever', 'Synchronicity', 'Outlandos D'Amour'
6   'King Creole', 'The Young Ones', 'GI Blues', 'Love Me Tender'
7   Kraftwerk, Yellow Magic Orchestra, Trio, Scorpions
8   'Imagine', 'Aladdin Sane', 'Bridge Over Troubled Water'
9   'Baker Street', 'Finchley Central', 'Portsmouth', 'Angel'
10 'Fernando', 'Dancing Queen', 'Does Your Mother Know?'

 **B**

1 Neil MacArthur, Peter Fenton, Colin Blunstone
2 HMV, Decca, Columbia, Parlophone
3 UB40, Monkees, Kraftwerk
4 Ronnie Hilton, Lee Marvin, Captain Sensible, Gerry and the Pacemakers
5 Carpenters, Dollar, Nino Tempo and April Stevens
6 Bee Gees, Walker Brothers, Kalin Twins, Equals
7 Bee Gees, Earth Wind and Fire, Maurice Williams and the Zodiacs, Wings
8 Andy, Billy, Danny, David, Deniece, Diana, Don, Elvis, Iris, John, Kenny, Larry, Lenny, Mason, Maurice.
9 Move, Electric Light Orchestra, Slade, Wizzard
10 Electric Light Orchestra, Donna Summer, Cliff Richard, John Travolta

 **C**

1 Ian Dury, David Dundas, Nina and Frederick
2 Jim Reeves, Classix Nouveaux, Bob Dylan, Mike Oldfield
3 Charlie Drake, Benny Hill, Domenico Modugno, Dean Martin
4 Kate Robbins, Stephanie de Sykes, Des O'Connor, John Leyton
5 John Leyton, Ringo Starr, Gene Pitney, Tommy Edwards
6 'Jealous Guy' by Roxy Music, 'Prince Charming' by Adam and the Ants, 'Japanese Boy' by Aneka
7 Dana, Lulu, Aneka, Severine
8 'Don't Cry For Me Argentina', 'Amazing Grace', 'Annie's Song', 'If You Leave Me Now'
9 Marty Wilde, Frank Sinatra, Ronnie Hilton, Nat 'King' Cole
10 Peter Sellers, Siouxsie and The Banshees, Gene Pitney, Ella Fitzgerald

| QUIZ 59 | I'M GONNA SIT RIGHT DOWN AND WRITE MYSELF A LETTER |

Another word puzzle for you, to be completed like Quiz 18.

A   Author of the lyric you are looking for (3,5)

— — —/— — — — —

B   The same author's 1969 top five hit (3,4,3)
    __ __ __/__ __ __/__ __ __

C   First word in title of album containing quotation (7)
    __ __ __ __ __ __ __

D   Follow-up to hit containing quotation (10, 6, 6)
    __ __ __ __ __ __ __ __ __ __/__ __ __ __ __ __/
    __ __ __ __ __ __

E   They sang with Donna Summer on 'Unconditional
    Love'(7, 5) __ __ __ __ __ __ __/__ __ __ __ __

F   The longest-running number one of 1969 (5, 5)
    __ __ __ __ __/__ __ __ __ __

G   The record business measures sales in terms of these (5)
    __ __ __ __ __

H   Brian Epstein put the Beatles into these (5) __ __ __ __ __

I   Acronym in title of chart artist David McCallum's 1960s TV
    series (5) __ __ __ __ __

J   The Talking Heads burned this down in 1983 (5)
    __ __ __ __ __

K   Frankie Laine's first top ten hit (4, 4) __ __ __ __/__ __ __ __

L   Their 'Ying Tong Song' hit the top ten twice (3, 5)
    __ __ __/__ __ __ __ __

M   Nickname for *Cruisin'* DJ Arnie Ginsberg (3, 3)
    __ __ __/__ __ __

N   After Dusty Springfield closed her eyes, she began to do
    this (5) __ __ __ __ __

O   Media figure and Clash cohort Caroline (4) __ __ __ __

P   The kind of vibrations the Beach Boys preferred (4)
    __ __ __ __

Q   First word in title of Atkinson-Jones-Smith-Stephenson LP
    smash (3) __ __ __

R   For whom did Paul McCartney sing on 'Revolver'? (2, 3)
    __ __/__ __ __

S   1971 Brenda and the Tabulations soul hit, 'Right on the
    Tip of My __ __ __ __ __ __' (6)

T   Johnny Mathis' 1979 success, 'Gone __ __ __ __/__ __ __ __
    (4, 4)

U   Steve Martin rhapsodized about this King (3) __ __ __

V   What the Who could do for miles (3) __ __ __

W   Dave, Joey and Kiki had this in common (3) __ __ __

X   First four utterances in Freeez hit 'I.O.U.' (4) __ __ __ __

Y   One of Bill Haley's group (5) __ __ __ __ __

Z   Three of these made a Damned good record (4)
    __ __ __ __

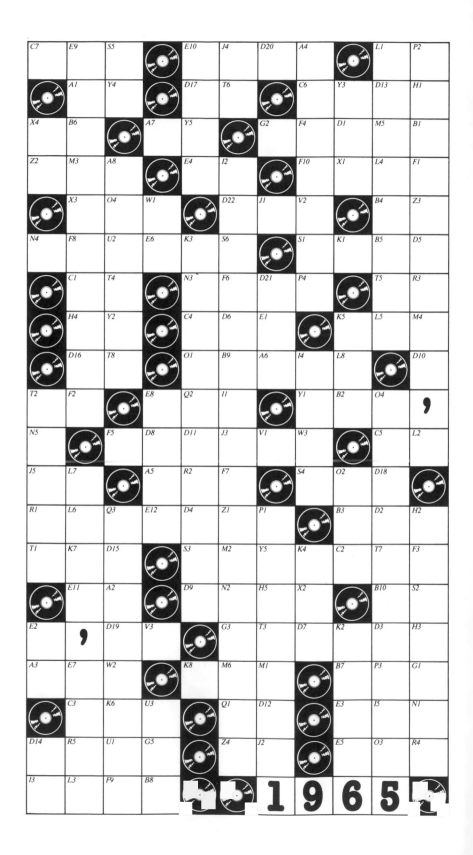

| QUIZ 60 | SPACE ODDITY |

1 Who did the 'Moon Hop'?
2 Who went to Jupiter?
3 Where did Sheer Elegance date their pretty baby?
4 What was it that was first recorded during Roman times, inspired the name of a rock 'n' roll band and is scheduled to return in 1985?
5 Who discovered an important note from space?
6 Who wanted to have her baby on Mars?
7 Who warned "Neptune, Titan, stars can frighten you"?
8 Curved Air were the mentors of this group.
9 In which song would you find the words "Jai Guru Dg Va Om"?
10 Who was 2000 light years from home?

| QUIZ 61 | STRANGER IN PARADISE |

This quiz gives clues to the identity of 45 acts who enjoyed chart success as a secondary career. Most would never have dared dream of achieving a hit record. If you get them all right you really should compile the next edition of *Who's Who*.

1 The lolly lover who earned bread with Bread
2 These TV kids found fame just as they claimed they would
3 The US sergeant who sang about his fellow Green Berets
4 The grandfatherly actor who sang about a grandad
5 He rapped on the door of the Top Ten in the best possible taste
6 Ribald reggae gave this large crude wit four "big" hits
7 This Belgian became an overnight star with 'Dominique'
8 Puppets who made it more than halfway up the Top 20 in 1977
9 Dr Who who gummed up the chart in 1980
10 There was nothing fawlty with this comic's hit LPs

11 The actress whose exercise LP was a world hit

12 His Top 40 hit was alright . . . or was that alwright?

13 From TV to the Top 40 for this yellowcoat . . . hi de hi indeed!

14 This dance troupe partnered Sarah Brightman into the Top Ten

15 This Radio 2 megamouth did not receive floral tributes for his dance hit

 **B**

1 The opera superstar who duetted with John Denver

2 Chas and Dave helped this squad fulfil a Top Five dream

3 The only Prime Minister to have a Top Ten LP of speeches

4 It wasn't hard for this Rochdale cowboy to ride into the Top 30

5 This *Tiswas* team were among the first wets to chart

6 During the summer of 1965 this trend-setting comedian was in the Top 40 both as a soloist and as part of a duo

7 The only Radio 1 daytime DJ to reach the Top 40 twice

8 For this TV star to record with Connie Stevens was kookie

9 The beloved TV junkman and son made a hit that was no rubbish

10 This Anglo-French action duo recorded a steamy number one that didn't sound like acting

11 He enjoyed a chart bonanza with a song about a Western villain with a Beatle's name.

12 This Israeli stage star got rich by fiddling the charts

13 Apple Records helped these chanters become charters

14 Folk parodist whose 'Hello Muddah Hello Faddah' still gets radio play over two decades after its release

15 They had two hits twelve years apart, during which time the membership of this team had changed completely

 **C**

1 He won three Oscars but only one Top 40 place, that with a song about an ageing farmer

2 This nun took The Lord's Prayer into charts around the world

3 A live recording at the Oxford Union gave this comedian a Top Five LP

4 TV Beatle parodists who actually charted themselves

5   This Australian actor made the top forty with a song subtitled 'Tous Les Bateux, Tous Les Oiseaux'

6   Long before the Singing Sheep made their baad single these canines barked their way into the Top 20

7   Intellectual American satirist who found himself in Britain's first Top Ten LP list

8   Two disc jockeys found themselves in the Top Five parodying C W McCall

9   The businessman who made the American Top Ten with 'An Open Letter To My Teenage Son'

10 This actor got into the Top Ten in 1954 on the B-side of his wife

11 The esteemed BBC broadcaster reached the LP chart on the sheer strength of his 'Voice'

12 This American DJ ducked into the charts in 1976

13 Make the Top 20? "We can do it," this football team claimed, and they did.

14 The German children who wandered through the charts for 31 weeks in 1954

15 She roared into the 1961 charts with songs from the 20s

| QUIZ 62 | MERRY XMAS EVERYBODY |

Not to be attempted before December 25th

1   Which year were the following records Christmas time hits: Wah – 'Story Of The Blues', Culture Club – 'Time (Clock Of The Heart)', Jam – 'Beat Surrender'?

2   Who was 'Rockin' Around The Christmas Tree' in 1962?

3   Which two Americans sang about the 'Jingle Bell Rock'?

4   What did Dora Bryan want for Christmas?

5   Mud's second number one was a Christmas song. What was it?

6   Who wanted to 'Step Into Christmas' in 1973?

7   Where did Father Abraham spend Christmas in 1978?

8   Which seasonally named group could not resist the chance of making a Christmas song medley in 1981?

9   Who had a Xmas Party in 1982?

10 Who provided 'additional noises' on Wizzard's 1973 hit, 'I Wish It Could Be Christmas Everyday'?

 **B**

1 Which year were the following records Christmas-time hits: Beatles – 'Hello Goodbye', Dave Clark Five – 'Everybody Knows', Tom Jones – 'I'm Coming Home'?

2 Which two groups or artists have had British hits with the carol 'Silent Night'?

3 Elvis Presley's 1957 LP 'Elvis Sings Christmas Songs' included a Leiber-Stoller song which was eventually released as a single in 1980. What was it?

4 A former bass player with King Crimson made number two with a Christmas song. Who was he and what was the song?

5 In 1982 the Altar Boys brought out a Christmassy version of which rock 'n' roll classic?

6 Who was responsible for the novelty records 'Renta Santa' and 'Bionic Santa'?

7 Who recorded 'Frosty The Snowman' on the Phil Spector Christmas album?

8 Who reached number one with the 'Christmas Alphabet'?

9 Which children's choir featured on John and Yoko's 'Happy Christmas (War Is Over)'?

10 Fogwell Flax and the Anklebiters took the CB craze into the realm of Christmas songs with which song?

 **C**

1 Which year were the following records Christmas-time hits: Electric Light Orchestra – 'Living Thing', Queen – 'Somebody To Love', Showaddywaddy – 'Under The Moon Of Love'?

2 The Harry Simeone Chorale took which song into the US Top 30 five Christmasses running (1958–62)?

3 Rolling Stone Keith Richard has only released one solo single (to 1983) and it was a cover of Chuck Berry's Christmas novelty. What?

4 The Holly Twins recorded a song entitled 'I Want Elvis For Christmas'. Who played guitar and sang back-up vocals for them?

5 Several years ago the NME printed a review for an album 'Snow Over Interstate 80'. The album never appeared and there is little evidence to suggest it ever existed. Who was supposed to have recorded it?

6 Rudy and the Rialtos' single 'Christmas Tears Will Fall' featured a guest 'appearance' by which American DJ?

7 When was 'I'm Walking Backwards For Christmas' originally a British Hit for the Goons?

8 Whose first Christmas did Connie Francis sing about?

9 A live version of Slade's classic 'Merry Xmas Everybody' appeared as the B-Side to which of their later singles?

10 In December 1979 the Greedies had a hit with 'A Merry Jingle'. Who were the Greedies?

QUIZ 63	YOU KNOW MY NAME . . . LOOK UP MY NUMBER

For this quiz in our book you will have to flick back through the pages and look at the titles of the previous quizzes. Try to name the artists *most* associated with the 60 songs. All have been released as singles with the exception of one that is a well-known album track and one a B-side.

QUIZ 1
THE NAME GAME

 **A**

1 Peggy Sue
2 Jack
3 Joe
4 Jude
5 Paula
6 Johnny
7 John
8 Grace
9 Louie
10 Jake
11 Rosie
12 Sam
13 Ben
14 Sylvia
15 Joe
16 Annie
17 Arthur
18 Cathy
19 Julie
20 Ernie

 **B**

1 Mary Anne
2 Larry
3 Jane
4 Rita
5 Bridget the Midget
6 Debora
7 Jennifer
8 Rhonda
9 Lily
10 Caroline
11 Sherry
12 Delilah
13 Barbara
14 Annie
15 Susie
16 Liberty Valance
17 Georgie
18 Maggie
19 Pearl
20 Martha

 **C**

1 Lisa
2 Hercules
3 Ollie Vee
4 Annie
5 Cindy
6 Timothy
7 Billy
8 Little White Dove
9 Dominique
10 Mrs Brown
11 Judy
12 Mrs Jones
13 Henry VIII
14 Jet
15 Laurie
16 Sally
17 Maria
18 Harry Truman
19 Bobby
20 Lucretia MacEvil

QUIZ 2
WE ARE FAMILY

 **A**

1 Elvis Presley
2 Abba
3 There have been hits of this title by Dave Berry, Connie Francis, Genesis, and David Whitfield
4 Chicory Tip
5 Lonnie Donegan
6 Junior
7 Clive Dunn
8 Slade
9 James Brown
10 Pigbag
11 Temptations
12 St Winifred's School Choir
13 Paul Simon
14 Tom Jones
15 Shep and the Limelites, Jermaine Jackson and Cliff Richard all had success with this song
16 Hot Chocolate and Stories both had success with this song
17 Herman's Hermits
18 Boney M and Darts both charted with songs of this title
19 Dusty Springfield
20 Drifters

ANSWERS

 B

1 Vera Lynn
2 John Lennon
3 Eddie Calvert and Eddie Fisher both had success with this song
4 O C Smith
5 Intruders
6 Sister Sledge
7 Three Dog Night
8 Marmalade
9 Paul Nicholas
10 Neil Reid
11 Free
12 Undertones
13 Jackson Five
14 The Johnny Otis Show and Lena Zavaroni both had success with this song
15 Cat Stevens
16 Sly and the Family Stone
17 Rolling Stones
18 War
19 Elvis Presley
20 New World

 C

1 Eydie Gormé
2 Connie Francis
3 The Children of Tansley School
4 Nat 'King' Cole
5 Paul Petersen
6 Suzi Quatro
7 Joan Regan
8 Perry Como
9 Ernie K-Doe
10 Elton John
11 Sam Cooke
12 David Whitfield
13 Rick Wakeman or The Early Music Consort Directed by David Munrow
14 Gladys Knight and the Pips
15 C C S
16 Happenings
17 Jan Bradley
18 Doris Day and Johnnie Ray
19 Three Dog Night
20 Harry Belafonte

QUIZ 3
I'M JUST A SINGER IN A ROCK 'N' ROLL BAND

1   Nick Heyward
2   Limahl
3   Mick Jagger and Bill Wyman
4   Bryan Ferry
5   Debbie Harry
6   Marc Bolan
7   Peter Gabriel and Phil Collins
8   Frankie Valli
9   Frida and Agnetha
10 Steve Harley
11 Paul Jones
12 Philip Lynott
13 Peter Noone
14 Sting
15 Lionel Richie
16 Diana Ross
17 Roger Daltrey and Pete Townshend
18 All of them! Gary, John and Scott
19 Robert Plant
20 Paul McCartney, John Lennon, Ringo Starr and George Harrison

1   Paul Young
2   Billy Idol
3   Graham Bonnett
4   David Gates
5   Mama Cass
6   Midge Ure
7   Ian Gillan
8   Graham Gouldman
9   Eddy Grant
10 Les Gray
11 Justin Hayward
12 Kevin Keegan
13 Ben E King
14 Ian Hunter
15 Mike Nesmith
16 Steve Winwood
17 Roy Wood
18 Jon Anderson
19 Colin Blunstone including one under the pseudonym of Neil McArthur
20 David Grant

ANSWERS

 C

1 Len Barry
2 Robert Palmer and Elkie Brooks
3 Marvin Gaye
4 Eric Carmen
5 P P Arnold
6 Bill Nelson
7 Eddie Kendricks
8 John Foxx
9 Paul Da Vinci
10 Dave Edmunds
11 Nick Lowe
12 Dave Davies
13 Kirsty McColl
14 Chris Thompson
15 Keith Relf
16 Linda Ronstadt
17 Gerry Rafferty
18 Van Morrison
19 Charlie Harper
20 Neil Young or Stephen Stills

QUIZ 4

I KNOW WHAT I LIKE IN YOUR WARDROBE

 A

1 Roxy Music
2 The Beatles
3 Marty Robbins
4 Marvin Gaye
5 Elvis Costello
6 Haircut 100
7 Jess Conrad
8 Joe Bennett and the Sparkletones
9 St Cecilia
10 Raincoat

QUIZ 5
TRACKS OF MY TEARS

 **A**

1 Led Zeppelin, 'Led Zeppelin II'
2 John Lennon, 'Imagine'
3 Don McLean, 'American Pie'
4 Police, 'Reggatta de Blanc'
5 Elvis Presley, 'King Creole'
6 Rolling Stones, 'Sticky Fingers'
7 Simon and Garfunkel, 'Bridge Over Troubled Water'
8 Rod Stewart, 'Never A Dull Moment'
9 Elton John, 'Goodbye Yellow Brick Road'
10 Beatles, 'Please Please Me'
11 Crickets, 'The Chirping Crickets'
12 Fleetwood Mac, 'Rumours'
13 Abba, 'The Visitors'
14 Adam and The Ants, 'Prince Charming'
15 Beatles, 'With The Beatles'

 **B**

1 Love, 'Forever Changes'
2 Paul McCartney, 'Ram'
3 Meat Loaf, 'Dead Ringer'
4 Elvis Presley, 'Moody Blue'
5 Various Artists, 'Jesus Christ Superstar'
6 Queen, 'A Day At The Races'
7 Leo Sayer, 'Endless Flight'
8 Simon and Garfunkel, 'Sounds of Silence'
9 Squeeze, 'Cool For Cats'
10 Cat Stevens, 'Teaser And The Firecat'
11 Elton John, 'Too Low For Zero'
12 Human League, 'Dare'
13 Eurythmics, 'Sweet Dreams (Are Made Of This)'
14 Michael Jackson, 'Thriller'
15 Soft Cell, 'The Art Of Falling Apart'

 **C**

1 Telly Savalas, 'Savalas'
2 Janis Joplin, 'Pearl'
3 Jefferson Airplane, 'Surrealistic Pillow'
4 George Harrison, 'All Things Must Pass'
5 Bob Dylan, 'John Wesley Harding'
6 Dire Straits, 'Dire Straits'
7 Creedence Clearwater Revival, 'Cosmo's Factory'
8 Joe Cocker, 'Mad Dogs And Englishmen'
9 Eddie Cochran, 'Eddie Cochran Memorial Album'
10 Kate Bush, 'The Kick Inside'
11 Elvis Presley, 'Fun in Acapulco'
12 Alice Cooper, 'Billion Dollar Babies'
13 Nilsson, 'Nilsson Schmilsson'
14 Elvis Costello, 'Almost Blue'
15 Cliff Richard, 'Wired For Sound'

ANSWERS

QUIZ 6
NUMBER OF THE BEAST

 **A**

1	3
2	24
3	1000
4	2–4–6–8
5	1963
6	2
7	1
8	1
9	16
10	1–2–3
11	1 and 10 ('One in Ten')
12	1
13	50
14	8
15	2
16	5:15
17	7
18	16
19	3
20	18
21	59th
22	3
23	77
24	64
25	9
26	8th
27	19
28	16
29	96
30	9 to 5
31	8
32	98.6
33	1
34	5–4–3–2–1
35	17 (7 Teen)

 **B**

1	18
2	9
3	2
4	9 in 10 ('Nine Times Out Of Ten')
5	3rd
6	1
7	1 000 000 ('Never In A Million Years')
8	100
9	99
10	40
11	1
12	10538
13	137
14	12:30
15	6
16	8th
17	1000

18 16
19 40
20 5
21 4
22 3
23 48
24 5
25 1 ('One And One Is One')
26 ⅔ ('Two Out Of Three Ain't Bad')
27 1 ('One Of Us Must Know [Sooner or Later]')
28 634–5789
29 12 and 20 ('Twixt Twelve and Twenty')
30 747
31 7
32 1 ('One Inch Rock')
33 25
34 25, 6 and 4 ('25 or 6 to 4')
35 1 ('Fool Number One')

 C

1   40
2   7th
3   17
4   2
5   21
6   007
7   6
8   2
9   5
10 5 ('I've Got Five Dollars and It's Saturday Night')
11 8 By 10
12 2
13 7
14 7
15 5
16 6:00
17 2:10, 6:18 (10:44 was not listed in the title)
18 1
19 '65
20 17 ('Seventeen')
21 1 in 1 000 000 ('One In A Million You')
22 10 000
23 100
24 5
25 867–5309
26 3
27 60
28 7–6–5–4–3–2–1
29 4
30 7 (The Avons and Paul Evans both hit with 'Seven Little Girls Sitting In
        The Back Seat')
31 12
32 5, 10, 15, 20, 25, and 30 ('5–10–15–20 [25–30 Years of Love]')
33 6 000 000
34 7000
35 20

ANSWERS

QUIZ 7
THE END OR THE BEGINNING

A

1 Island, Status Quo, Blondie
2 Tango, Richard Myhill, Expressos
3 Missing, Chords, Selecter
4 Rebel, Matchbox Duane Eddy
5 Woman, Guess Who, Gary Puckett and the Union Gap
6 Tiger, Survivor, Mud
7 Party, Paul Nicholas, Associates
8 Do, Rods, Stevie Wonder
9 Mind, Anthony Newley, John Lennon
10 Golden, Tremeloes, David Bowie

B

1 Blue, Jeff Beck or Paul Mauriat or the Dells, New Order or Fats Domino
2 Get, Buzzcocks, Beatles or Rod Stewart
3 Dance, Love Sculpture, Dexy's Midnight Runners
4 Life, Depeche Mode, Eagles
5 Heartaches, Paul and Barry Ryan, Guy Mitchell
6 Moon, Connie Francis, Cat Stevens
7 Day, Father Abraham and the Smurfs, Beatles or Otis Redding
8 Boogie, T Rex, Heatwave
9 Train, Elvis Presley, Ethiopians
10 Young, Classix Nouveaux, Gary Puckett and the Union Gap

C

1 Two, Dave King, Rolf Harris
2 Child, Supremes, Kim Wilde
3 Rising, Cliff Richard, Medicine Head
4 Central, New Vaudeville Band, Thunderthighs
5 Midnight, Clodagh Rodgers, Pretty Things
6 Drums, Tony Sheveton, Sandy Nelson
7 Annie, Elvis Presley, Squeeze
8 Wheels, Wings, Slade
9 Pilot, Eric Burdon, Charlie Dore
10 Music, Bill Nelson's Red Noise, Imagination

QUIZ 8
YOU'LL ALWAYS FIND ME IN THE KITCHEN AT PARTIES

1 'Shake Rattle And Roll'
2 Fortunes
3 In the pantry
4 'What Could Be Nicer'
5 John Leyton
6 Toast and marmalade
7 Limmie and Family Cookin'
8 'I'd Have Baked A Cake'
9 Main Ingredient
10 'Toast'

QUIZ 9
OVER UNDER SIDEWAYS DOWN

1 'Gamblin' Man' by Lonnie Donegan
2 'All I Have To Do Is Dream' by the Everly Brothers
3 'Stupid Cupid' by Connie Francis
4 'One Night' by Elvis Presley
5 'Rivers Of Babylon' by Boney M
6 'Too Shy' by Kajagoogoo
7 'His Latest Flame' by Elvis Presley
8 'Reach For The Stars' by Shirley Bassey
9 'The Next Time' by Cliff Richard
10 'A Fool Such As I' by Elvis Presley
11 'Day Tripper' by the Beatles
12 'Eleanor Rigby' by the Beatles
13 'Rock-A-Hula Baby' by Elvis Presley
14 'I Don't Want To Talk About It' by Rod Stewart
15 'What A Wonderful World' by Louis Armstrong
16 'Candy Girl' by New Edition.
17 'Rock Your Baby' by George McCrae
18 'Daydreamer' by David Cassidy
19 'Cathy's Clown' by the Everly Brothers
20 'A Town Called Malice' by the Jam
21 'Mull of Kintyre' by Wings
22 'The Model' by Kraftwerk
23 'I Don't Wanna Dance' by Eddie Grant
24 'Going Underground' by the Jam
25 'Magic Moments' by Perry Como

ANSWERS

 **B**

1. 'True' by Spandau Ballet
2. 'Let's Dance' by David Bowie
3. 'Beat Surrender' by the Jam
4. 'Do You Really Want To Hurt Me' by Culture Club
5. 'Fame' by Irene Cara
6. 'Start' by the Jam
7. 'Cum On Feel The Noize' by Slade
8. 'Je T'Aime . . . Moi Non Plus' by Jane Birkin and Serge Gainsbourg
9. 'Honky Tonk Women' by the Rolling Stones
10. 'The Ballad of John And Yoko' by the Beatles
11. 'Get Back' by the Beatles
12. 'Hey Jude' by the Beatles
13. 'A Whiter Shade Of Pale' by Procol Harum
14. 'Help' by the Beatles
15. 'I Want To Hold Your Hand' by the Beatles
16. 'Karma Chameleon' by Culture Club
17. 'Is There Something I Should Know' by Duran Duran
18. 'Satisfaction' by the Rolling Stones
19. 'The Last Time' by the Rolling Stones
20. 'Jailhouse Rock' by Elvis Presley
21. 'Way Down' by Elvis Presley
22. 'It Doesn't Matter Anymore' by Buddy Holly
23. 'That'll Be The Day' by the Crickets
24. 'Bad Moon Rising' by Creedence Clearwater Revival
25. 'Are You Lonesome Tonight' by Elvis Presley

 **C**

1. 'The Wonder Of You' by Elvis Presley
2. 'Foot Tapper' by the Shadows
3. 'Israelites' by Desmond Dekker and the Aces
4. 'Lady Madonna' by the Beatles
5. 'Mighty Quinn' by Manfred Mann
6. 'San Francisco' (Be Sure To Wear Some Flowers In Your Hair) by Scott McKenzie. The song was also the original A-side to 'Maggie May' by Rod Stewart which later became the main track
7. 'Paperback Writer' by the Beatles
8. 'King Of The Road' by Roger Miller
9. 'Somebody Help Me' by the Spencer Davis Group
10. 'She Loves You' by the Beatles
11. 'Temptation' by the Everly Brothers
12. 'You're Driving Me Crazy' by the Temperance Seven
13. 'Poetry In Motion' by Johnny Tillotson
14. 'Singing The Blues' by Tommy Steele
15. 'Wherever I Lay My Hat' by Paul Young
16. 'Baby Jane' by Rod Stewart
17. 'You Can't Hurry Love' by Phil Collins
18. 'House Of Fun' by Madness
19. 'I Heard It Through The Grapevine' by Marvin Gaye
20. 'Goody Two Shoes' by Adam Ant
21. 'Barbados' by Typically Tropical
22. 'Use It Up And Wear It Out' by Odyssey
23. 'House Of The Rising Sun' by the Animals
24. 'Needles and Pins' by the Searchers
25. 'Diana' by Paul Anka

QUIZ 10
NUMBER ONE SONG IN HEAVEN

1 Deniece Williams
2 Meco
3 'Fame'
4 'If I Can't Have You' by Yvonne Elliman
5 '(Sittin' on) The Dock Of The Bay'
6 'Grazing In The Grass'
7 'Mrs Robinson'
8 'I'm A Believer'
9 'This Guy's In Love With You'
10 'You're Sixteen'
11 'Rock Me Gently'
12 'The First Time Ever I Saw Your Face'
13 'I Want You Back'
14 'Mack The Knife'
15 'He's So Fine' by the Chiffons
16 'Grease'
17 'Raindrops Keep Falling On My Head'
18 'The Tears Of A Clown'
19 'Penny Lane'
20 96
21 'I Heard It Through The Grapevine'
22 'Flashdance . . . What A Feeling'
23 'Big Bad John'
24 The Police, 'Every Breath You Take'
25 'House Of The Rising Sun'
26 'Eye Of The Tiger', Survivor
27 'Whatever Gets You Through The Night'
28 'Lucy In The Sky With Diamonds'
29 'My Girl'
30 'No More Tears'

1 'Centerfold' by the J Geils Band
2 'The Sound Of Philadelphia'
3 Marilyn McCoo and Billy Davis, Jr, 'You Don't Have To Be A Star (To Be In My Show)'
4 'Car Wash'
5 'I Write The Songs' (The song was written by Bruce Johnston.)
6 'Welcome Back'
7 'Dancing Queen'
8 'Love Is Blue'
9 'Killing Me Softly With His Song'
10 'Love Theme From *Romeo And Juliet*'
11 'Uncle Albert/Admiral Halsey'
12 'You've Lost That Lovin' Feelin''
13 'Are You Lonesome Tonight'
14 'He's a Rebel,' the Crystals
15 The Singing Nun, 'Dominique'
16 'Hey Jude'
17 'The Wayward Wind'
18 The Chipmunks, 'The Chipmunk Song'
19 'Heartbreak Hotel'
20 Jan and Dean, 'Surf City'

ANSWERS

21   'The Love You Save'
22   'Someday We'll Be Together'
23   'Crazy Little Thing Called Love' and 'Another One Bites The Dust'
24   Superman and Green Lantern
25   'Ben' by Michael Jackson
26   Stevie Wonder, 'Sir Duke'
27   'Breaking Up Is Hard To Do'
28   'Escape' by Rupert Holmes
29   Zager and Evans, 'In The Year 2525'
30   'Back In My Arms Again'

 C

1   'Love Will Keep Us Together' by the Captain and Tennille
2   Freddy Fender, 'Before The Next Teardrop Falls'
3   'Saturday Night'
4   'The Twist' by Chubby Checker
5   'El Paso' by Marty Robbins
6   'Auf Wiederseh'n Sweetheart' by Vera Lynn
7   Louis Armstrong, 'Hello Dolly'
8   Jimmy Gilmer
9   'Sukiyaki' by Kyu Sakamoto
10   The Highwaymen, 'Michael'
11   'Go Away Little Girl,' Donny Osmond
12   Strawberry Alarm Clock, 'Incense and Peppermints'
13   Dave Bartholomew
14   'Candy Man,' Sammy Davis, Jr.
15   'Tammy', Debbie Reynolds
16   'Cherry Pink And Apple Blossom White' by Perez Prado
17   'Patricia'
18   'Fingertips Pt 2' by Little Stevie Wonder
19   'Green Door' by Jim Lowe
20   'Purple People Eater' by Sheb Wooley
21   'Sixteen Tons' by Tennessee Ernie Ford
22   Larry Verne
23   'Let Me Go Lover' by Joan Weber
24   'Coming Up' by Paul McCartney and Wings
25   'Pop Musik' by M
26   The Arrows
27   'Another Somebody Done Somebody Wrong Song'
28   'Hearts of Stone'
29   'Still'
30   'Nel Blu Dipinto Di Blu'

QUIZ 11
IT'S ONLY ROCK 'N' ROLL

1 Procul Harum with 'A Whiter Shade Of Pale'.
2 They both had hits with pop versions of songs from Broadway shows; 'America' from *West Side Story* and 'Happy Talk' from *South Pacific*
3 Mason Williams
4 'Tahiti'
5 B Bumble and the Stingers who called their version 'Nut Rocker'
6 The William Tell Overture by Rossini
7 'Whisky In The Jar'
8 'Chi Mai' (the theme from the BBC TV Series *The Life And Times Of*

1 Khatchaturian
2 The Royal Philharmonic Orchestra
3 'Pictures At An Exhibition'
4 'Book Of Invasions (A Celtic Symphony)'
5 *Evita* by Tim Rice and Andrew Lloyd Webber
6 Jupiter
7 Jon Lord
8 'Chi Mia' (the theme from the BBC TV Series *The Life And Times Of David Lloyd George*)

1 'Amazing Grace' by The Pipes and Drums and Military Band of the Royal Scots Dragoon Guards.
2 The London Symphony Orchestra
3 Rodrigo's Guitar Concerto De Aranjuez (Theme From 2nd Movement) by Manuel and his Music of the Mountains.
4 Swan Lake
5 Nero & the Gladiators
6 Soft Machine
7 The Piltdown Men
8 'The Quartermaster's Stores'

QUIZ 12
A PICTURE OF YOU

1 Denny Laine is the batsman. The fielder is Clint Warwick and they were replaced in the Moody Blues by John Lodge and Justin Hayward
2 John Lennon
3 Reg Presley of The Troggs
4 Scott Walker
5 Georgie Fame
6 Engelbert Humperdinck
7 John Dec and Con recorded on Decca as the Bachelors. Steve and Rikki recorded on Parlophone as Bachelors
8 He's Mickie Most and the wall carries some of the gold discs he has produced.
9 John Deacon of Queen
10 Marty Wilde

ANSWERS

QUIZ 13
I WRITE THE SONGS

 A

1 John Lennon
2 Gary Byrd & Stevie Wonder
3 Cat Stevens
4 John Denver
5 Neil Diamond
6 John Lennon & Paul McCartney
7 Eddie Grant
8 Roy Orbison
9 Mike Batt
10 John Lennon & Paul McCartney
11 Paul Anka
12 Joni Mitchell
13 Bob Dylan
14 Neil Diamond
15 Mick Jagger & Keith Richard
16 David Bowie
17 Bob Dylan
18 George Harrison
19 Jonathan King
20 John Lennon & Paul McCartney

 B

1 Melanie Safka
2 Johnny Bristol
3 Paul Anka
4 John Phillips
5 Jeff Barry & Andy Kim
6 Chris Andrews
7 Lionel Bart
8 Andrew Lloyd Webber
9 Gerry Goffin & Carole King
10 Hal David & Burt Bacharach
11 Berry Gordy Jnr
12 Cat Stevens
13 Jerry Lordan
14 John D Loudermilk
15 Barry & Robin Gibb
16 John Holt
17 John Lennon & Paul McCartney
18 Paul Ryan
19 Mike Batt
20 Bob Dylan

 C

1 Don Gibson
2 Sonny Curtis
3 John D Loudermilk
4 Lionel Bart
5 Merle Travis
6 P J Proby
7 Bruce Springsteen
8 Kirsty MacColl
9 Don McLean
10 Jimi Hendrix
11 Mick Jagger & Keith Richard
12 Mason Williams
13 Harry Nilsson
14 P F Sloan
15 Smokey Robinson
16 Gene Pitney
17 Gene Pitney
18 Tim Hardin
19 Don Everly
20 Hugo Peretti, Luigi Creatore, George David Weiss, Solomon Linda, Albert Stanton, Pete Seeger, Fred Hellerman, Lee Hayes and Ronnie Gilbert. (Anybody who gets this one right can have an extra point!)

QUIZ 14

THREE STEPS TO HEAVEN

1 Rolling Stones
2 Rascals (a.k.a. Young Rascals)
3 Sham 69
4 Donna Summer
5 Beatles
6 Boomtown Rats
7 Pat Boone
8 Bobby Darin
9 Shalamar
10 Duran Duran
11 Earth Wind and Fire
12 Bob Dylan
13 Sheena Easton
14 Ian Dury and the Blockheads
15 Dion
16 Rose Royce
17 David Bowie

18 Elton John
19 Tommy James and the Shondells
20 Michael Jackson
21 Tony Bennett
22 Gilbert O'Sullivan
23 Roy Orbison
24 O'Jays
25 Nilsson
26 Peggy Lee
27 Jerry Lee Lewis
28 Gladys Knight and the Pips
29 Gary Puckett and the Union Gap
30 UB40

ANSWERS

QUIZ 15
SILLY LOVE SONGS

 **A**

1 Brian Hyland
2 Charlie Drake
3 Joe Dolce Music Theatre (Joe Dolce will do)
4 Renee & Renato
5 David Bowie
6 The Beatles
7 Chuck Berry
8 Benny Hill
9 Billy Connolly
10 Scaffold
11 The Tweets
12 Trio
13 Ohio Express
14 Wayne Fontana & The Mindbenders (Major Lance, who had the
original US hit but only a minor one in the UK, also correct)
15 Meri (not Mari) Wilson

 **B**

1 Ray Stevens with 'The Streak'
2 'Brand New Key'
3 The Bonzo Dog Doo-Dah Band, later known just as the Bonzo Dog
Band
4 Bernard Cribbins
5 Laurence Olivier as Richard III reading 'A Hard Days Night'
6 Peter Sellers with Sophia Loren
7 Splodgenessabounds
8 The Barron Knights
9 The Rockin' Berries
10 Lieutenant Pigeon
11 Jim Stafford
12 They were all Ross Bagdasarian, creator of the Chipmunks (Alvin,
Simon and Theodore), producer of 'The Trouble With Harry' (a disc
credited to Alfi and Harry) and recording artist under the name
David Seville. His one UK hit as Seville was the novelty 'Witch
Doctor'.
13 Roger Miller
14 Nephew. He is Robin the Frog.
15 Bobby Crush

C

1 'Short People', Randy Newman
2 'Western Movies', Olympics
3 'Monster Mash', Bobby 'Boris' Pickett & The Crypt-Kickers
4 'Alley-Oop', Hollywood Argyles – other US hit versions were by Dante
& the Evergreens & the Dyna-Sores
5 'Cinderella Rockefella', Esther & Abi Ofarim
6 'Life Is A Rock (But The Radio Rolled Me)', Reunion
7 'Hello Muddah, Hello Fadduh!', Allan Sherman
8 'In The Mood', Henhouse Five Plus Too (Ray Stevens as chickens)
9 'How Much Is That Doggie In The Window', Lita Roza (UK) or Patti
Page (US)

10 'Je T'Aime (Moi Non Plus)', Jane Birkin & Serge Gainsbourg
11 'Wikka Rap', Evasions (vocal was an impression of Alan Whicker)
12 'There's A Guy Works Down The Chipshop Swears He's Elvis', Kirsty McColl
13 'Hello This Is Joanie (The Telephone Answering Machine Song)', Paul Evans
14 'All I Want For Christmas Is A Beatle', Dora Bryan
15 'Tie Me Kangaroo Down Sport', Rolf Harris

QUIZ 16
SPLISH SPLASH

1 Buggles
2 The Beat
3 'A Little Bit Of Soap'
4 Pink and blue
5 'Ain't Gonna Wash For A Week'
6 CCS
7 'She Came In Through The Bathroom Window'
8 'Mr Clean'
9 'Rub A Dub Dub'
10 'The Water Is Over My Head'

QUIZ 17
DEDICATED TO THE ONE I LOVE

1 Elvis Presley, 'I Remember Elvis Presley'
2 John Wayne, 'John Wayne Is Big Leggy'
3 Buddy Holly, 'Tribute To Buddy Holly'
4 Elvis Presley, 'There's A Guy Works Down The Chip Shop Swears He's Elvis', by Kirsty McColl
5 Geno Washington, 'Geno'
6 Vincent van Gogh, 'Vincent'
7 Abraham Lincoln, 'Abraham, Martin and John'
8 David Lloyd George
9 Bonnie and Clyde
10 Al Capone
11 'Alexander Graham Bell', by Sweet
12 Eva Peron, 'Don't Cry For Me, Argentina' from Evita
13 Osvaldo Ardiles, 'Ossie's Dream', by Tottenham Hotspur FC
14 A Beatle, 'All I Want For Christmas Is A Beatle'
15 Eddie Cochran, 'Just Like Eddie'
16 John Lennon, with whom Elton John had a small hit with 'I Saw Her Standing There'
17 Marilyn Monroe
18 Bette Davis 'Bette Davis Eyes'
19 Baron von Richtofen, 'Return Of The Red Baron'
20 John Lennon

ANSWERS

 **B**

1. L S Lowry, 'Matchstalk Men and Matchstalk Cats And Dogs'
2. Buddy Holly, Big Bopper, Ritchie Valens
3. General George Custer, 'Mr Custer'
4. Jim Reeves, 'Tribute To Jim Reeves'
5. George Best
6. Julian Lennon. It started life as 'Hey Jules'
7. Anne Deutschendorf, wife of John Denver (real name Deutschendorf)
8. Patti D'arbanville, 'Lady D'arbanville'
9. Otis Redding, 'Tribute To A King'
10. Martin Luther King
11. Christine Keeler 'Christine', by Miss X
12. Cyril Knowles, 'Nice One, Cyril'
13. Roger McGuinn and Barry McGuire
14. Peter Brown, 'Ballad Of John And Yoko'
15. Laurel & Hardy. (Their hit was 'Trail Of The Lonesome Pine'; the Equals hit with 'Laurel and Hardy')
16. John Lennon
17. 'Davy Crockett' (It was a hit for Max Bygraves, Bill Hayes, Dick James and Tennessee Ernie Ford)
18. Don McLean
19. Rudy Pompilli, saxophonist with Haley's Comets
20. Queen Elizabeth II, on the way to her coronation

 **C**

1. Princess Margaret and Lord Snowdon
2. Clair Mills, daughter of his then manager, Gordon Mills
3. Johnny Cash. ('The Folk Singer', by Tommy Roe, hit no. 4 in 63)
4. Elvis Presley
5. Reuben 'Hurricane' Carter, a boxer imprisoned for murder
6. Buddy Holly died. The bad news was the report of the plane crash.
7. Jackie Wilson, 'Jackie Wilson Said'
8. Paul McCartney
9. Guy Burchett, messenger at Rocket Records who was killed in a motorcyle accident, aged 17
10. Carole King
11. Clyde McPhatter, one time lead singer of the Drifters, who was present at the 'Ahab The Arab' session
12. Berry Gordy
13. The Belmonts, in the Four Preps pastiche of 'Teenager In Love'.
14. Adam Faith. "You can make more money writing Adam Faith songs" is what Donegan sings
15. Joan Of Arc, 'Joan Of Arc' and 'Maid Of Orleans'
16. Frank Lloyd Wright, 'So Long Frank Lloyd Wright'
17. Stevie Wonder's baby daughter. The song was written by Wonder
18. Robert F Kennedy
19. Scott Davis, young son of songwriter Mac Davis
20. Bob Wills, often called 'the king of Western Swing'. Waylon Jennings' song was called 'Bob Wills Is Still The King'

I'M GONNA SIT RIGHT DOWN AND WRITE MYSELF A LETTER

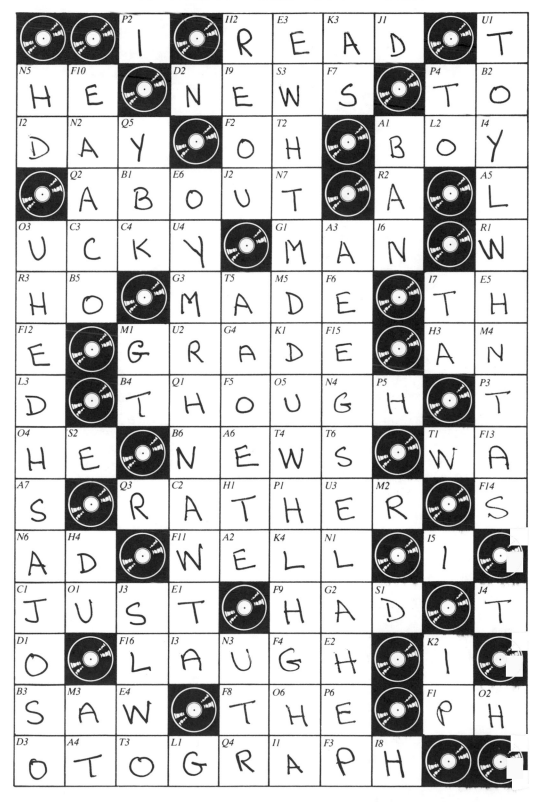

ANSWERS

QUIZ 19
MISSING WORDS

 **A**

1 '(Hey There) . . .'
2 '. . . (Man It Was Mean)'
3 '. . . (And Super Creeps)'
4 '. . . (Knock Yourself Out)'
5 '. . . (Boy Meets Girl)'
6 '(I Don't Want To Go To) . . .'
7 '. . . (Finger On The Trigger)'
8 '. . . (Don't Hurt Me)'
9 '(You're) . . .'
10 '. . . (Everything's Alright)'
11 '. . . (Where My Rosemary Goes)'
12 '(Dancing) . . .'
13 '. . . (From The Start)'
14 '. . . (Till I Saw You Rock N Roll)'
15 '(Just Like) . . .'

 B

1 '(Get A) . . . (On Yourself)'
2 '. . . (Has Made A Loser Out Of Me)'
3 '. . . (Set Me Free)'
4 '. . . (What I Hear?)'
5 '. . . (Give Me Peace On Earth)'
6 '(No More) . . .'
7 '. . . (Be Sure To Wear Flowers in Your Hair)'
8 '. . . (It's Just A Story)'
9 '. . . (Spurs Are On Their Way To Wembley)'
10 '. . . (Shine On Me)'
11 '(Your Love Keeps Lifting Me) . . .'
12 '. . . (The Letter Song)'
13 '. . . (Something's Gonna Happen Tonight)'
14 '. . . (The Mood I'm In)'
15 '. . . (Birdie Dance)'

 **C**

1 '. . . (Metal Postcard)'
2 '(And Now – The Waltz) . . .'
3 '. . . (Bebopafunkadiscolypso)'
4 '. . . (Holy Moses)'
5 '. . . (To Watch Good Love Go Bad)'
6 '. . . (Dog Ziggity Boom)'
7 '(I Washed My Hands In) . . .'
8 '. . . (Is It You?)'
9 '. . . (Can't Hide From Love)'
10 '. . . (Who Have Nothing)'
11 '. . . (Can't Live Without You)'
12 '. . . (Let Me Go)'
13 '. . . (Hooked On Love)'
14 '. . . (It's Got Me Caught In The Spotlight)'
15 '. . . (Don't Ya Jes Love It)'

QUIZ 20
WORKING ON A BUILDING OF LOVE

 **A**

1 The Jam
2 'Unhalfbricking'
3 Walls
4 'Bridge of Sighs'
5 John Foxx
6 Pretenders with 'Brass In Pocket'
7 'Concrete And Clay', a number one hit for Unit Four Plus Two and a
   hit for Randy Edelman 1976
8 C – 41
9 Steel Men
10 Genesis

QUIZ 21
COME TOGETHER

The gaps are filled in as follows:

Elkie Brooks; Chris Rea; Minnie Riperton; Brighouse & Rastrick Brass Band; Terry Wogan; Kathy Kirby; Teresa Brewer; Buddy Holly; The Beatles; Scaffold; The Four Bucketeers; The Specials (the track was 'Long Shot Kick De Bucket'); Funboy Three; Al Martino; Andy Williams; Survivor (the films were *Rocky*, *Rocky II* and *Rocky III*); Ides Of March.

1   Both hit number two, their biggest hits, with songs by Charlie Chaplin. The songs were 'Smile' for Nat King Cole and 'This Is My Song' for Harry Secombe
2   Both hit with 'This Is My Song'
3   Both starred in the film *Vice Versa* as child stars
4   Both hit number one with Lionel Bart Songs, 'Living Doll' for Cliff and 'Do You Mind' for Anthony Newley
5   Cliff has recorded various Buddy Holly tracks during his career, notably 'True Love Ways' which he took into the Top Ten in 1983
6   Mike Berry recorded 'Tribute To Buddy Holly'
7   Both starred in the BBC TV series, *Are You Being Served?*
8   Wendy Richard was the girl on Mike Sarne's 'Come Outside'
9   Billie Davis was the girl on Mike Sarne's 'Will I What?'
10 Both recorded 'Tell Him'
11 The Exciters made the original of 'Doo Wah Diddy Diddy', the Manfred Mann number one hit
12 Manfred Mann recorded two Dylan songs as single A-sides, 'If You Gotta Go, Go Now' and 'Mighty Quinn'
13 They co-wrote 'I'd Have You Anytime' on Harrison's 'All Things Must Pass' triple album
14 They were both Beatles
15 They hit number one world-wide with 'Ebony and Ivory'
16 They were at one time married
17 They recorded 'With You I'm Born Again' together
18 They have both hit the charts both vocally and with instrumental hits
19 They have both recorded James Bond themes. Herb Alpert recorded 'Casino Royale' and Carly Simon hit with 'Nobody Does It Better'
20 They married in 1972
21 James Taylor's biggest British hit, 'You've Got A Friend' was written by Carole King
22 Neil Sedaka recorded 'Oh Carol' about her
23 The Captain and Tennille recorded Sedaka's 'Love Will Keep Us Together'.

ANSWERS

24 Both have had singles with the word 'Muskrat' in the title. The Captain and Tennille took 'Muskrat Love' to number four in America. The Everly Brothers' 'Muskrat' reached number 20 in the UK late in 1961.

25 Both had a hit with 'Walk Right Back.'

26 Perry Como's hit 'And I Love You So' was written by Don McLean

27 Don McLean's number one 'Crying' was co-written and originally recorded by Roy Orbison

28 Glen Campbell played on most of Roy Orbison's early hits during his time as one of the highest paid session men in America

29 Glen Campbell is one of four people to have turned 'It's Only Make Believe', by Conway Twitty and Jack Nance, into a top ten hit in UK. Conway Twitty was the first.

30 They share a birthday, 1 September

31 Frankie Valli sang the title song for *Grease*, which was a Gibb composition.

32 Frankie Valli was lead singer for the Four Seasons on most of their British hits

33 Terry Jacks' biggest hit was 'Seasons In The Sun'.

34 Terry Jacks was a member of the Poppy Family. His then wife Susan sang lead on their big hit, 'Which Way Are You Going Billy?'

35 Paper Lace had another 'Billy' song, 'Billy Don't Be A Hero', which was a number one in England

36 Together they recorded a hit

37 That hit was a version of Laurie London's 'He's Got The Whole World In His Hands'. Paper Lace and Nottingham Forest F.C. rather less modestly recorded it as 'We've Got The Whole World In Our Hands'

38 Both had number one hits in America well before the Beatles invasion. Vera Lynn's was 'Auf Wiederseh'n Sweetheart', Laurie London's was the above-mentioned 'He's Got The Whole World In His Hands'.

39 Eddie Calvert was a co-writer of Vera Lynn's British number one, 'My Son, My Son'.

40 Both had a hit with 'Zambesi'.

41 So did Lou Busch.

42 They were one and the same person.

43 Both have hit the charts under two names, Colin Blunstone's other hit name being Neil MacArthur.

44 Blunstone was lead singer for the Zombies.

45 Rod Argent, founder of Argent, is another ex-Zombie.

46 Both have had hits with (different) songs called 'Tragedy'.

47 Dionne Warwick's hit LP and single 'Heartbreaker' was Bee Gee written and Barry Gibb produced.

48 Dionne Warwick had an earlier hit entitled 'Do You Know The Way To San José'.

49 Both had hits with the theme music from World Cup TV programmes, San José for BBC TV in 1978, and Jeff Wayne for ITV in 1982

50 David Essex starred in Jeff Wayne's massive smash LP, 'Jeff Wayne's War Of The Worlds'

51 Both had hits with 'Stardust', although they were different songs.

The answers given above are the ones we are looking for, but it is quite possible that you can find entirely acceptable other connections.

QUIZ 22
I'M IN THE MOOD FOR DANCING

 **A**

1 Roxy Music
2 Drifters
3 Sly and the Family Stone
4 Chris Montez
5 David Bowie
6 Men Without Hats
7 Wilson Pickett (or Cannibal and the Headhunters)
8 Sister Sledge
9 Marshall Hain
10 Martha and the Vandellas
11 Abba
12 Chubby Checker
13 Sam Cooke, Rod Stewart
14 Chubby Checker
15 Roxy Music
16 Chic
17 Coast to Coast
18 Beatles (or Isley Brothers, or Brian Poole and the Tremeloes)
19 Bobby Boris Pickett and the Crypt Kickers
20 Van McCoy

 **B**

1 Shadows (or Kathy Kirby or Mojo)
2 Dexy's Midnight Runners
3 Carl Douglas
4 Cozy Powell
5 Duane Eddy
6 Drifters (or Orleans with a different song of the same name)
7 Liquid Gold
8 Thin Lizzy
9 Third World
10 Paul Nicholas
11 Elvis Costello
12 Chubby Checker
13 Dee Dee Sharp
14 Bob and Earl
15 Edyie Gormé
16 Rufus Thomas
17 Elvis Presley
18 Showaddywaddy (or Chubby Checker)
19 Cliff Richard (or Bobby Freeman, Barry Blue, or Bette Midler; also Beach Boys or Mamas and Papas)
20 Chic (or Beach Boys)

ANSWERS

 C

1	Tina Charles	11	Alvin Cash and the Crawlers
2	Osibisa	12	Bobby Freeman
3	Danny Williams	13	Major Lance (or Tubes)
4	Voggue	14	Marvin Gaye
5	Motors	15	Tommy Dorsey Orchestra Starring Warren Covington
6	Atmosfear	16	Dee Dee Sharp (or Vernons Girls)
7	Rose Royce	17	Elvis Presley
8	Orlons	18	Fatback Band
9	Larks	19	Barron Knights
10	Miracles	20	Saturday Night Band

QUIZ 23
ONE AND ONE IS ONE

 A

1 No More + Heroes = No More Heroes
2 It's All Over Now + Baby Blue = It's All Over Now Baby Blue
3 Come On + Let's Go = Come On Let's Go
4 Crying + Over You = Crying Over You
5 Hurt + So Good = Hurt So Good
6 I Got You + Babe = I Got You Babe
7 I Love You + Because = I Love You Because
8 I Wonder + Why = I Wonder Why
9 Let's Go + Disco = Let's Go Disco
10 Lonely + Days = Lonely Days
11 Magic + Touch = Magic Touch
12 Man + Out Of Time = Man Out Of Time
13 Money + Honey = Money Honey
14 My Boy + Lollipop = My Boy Lollipop
15 Night + Fever = Night Fever

B

1 Angie + B-A-B-Y = Angie Baby
2 Belfast + Boy = Belfast Boy
3 Cry + My Heart = Cry My Heart
4 Don't + Answer Me = Don't Answer Me
5 Get Down + Tonight = Get Down Tonight
6 Get It + Together = Get It Together
7 Gypsy + Woman = Gypsy Woman
8 Heartache + Tonight = Heartache Tonight

9   I Can't Stop + Loving You = I Can't Stop Loving You
10   If + You Know What I Mean = If You Know What I Mean
11   Party + Time = Party Time
12   Rock On + Brother = Rock On Brother
13   Show Me + Girl = Show Me Girl
14   Somewhere + In The Country = Somewhere In The Country
15   What + Now = What Now

 C

1   Crazy + Water = Crazy Water
2   Everyday + People = Everyday People
3   Fallin' + In Love = Fallin' in Love
4   Goodnight + Midnight = Goodnight Midnight
5   Heart + Attack = Heart Attack
6   I Believe + You = I Believe You
7   Remember + When = Remember When
8   Start + Movin' = Start Movin'
9   Sunday + Girl = Sunday Girl
10   Too Much + Too Young = Too Much Too Young
11   You + Are Everything = You Are Everything
12   You + My Love = You My Love
13   Baby I Love You + OK = Baby I Love You OK
14   Just A Little Bit + Too Late = Just A Little Bit Too Late
15   Maybe + I Know = Maybe I Know

QUIZ 24
ON THE STREET WHERE YOU LIVE

 A

1   Eric Clapton
2   Maisonettes
3   'This Ole House'
4   'Penthouse and Pavement'
5   Severine with 'Un Banc Une Arbre et Une Rue' in 1971
6   'Marley Port Drive'
7   '24 Sycamore'
8   'Penny Lane'
9   'Blackberry Way'
10   Simon and Garfunkel in 'Sound of Silence'

ANSWERS

QUIZ 25
ALTERNATE TITLE

 **A**

1 'Then I Kissed Her'
2 'And Then She Kissed Me'
3 'Peggy Sue Got Married'
4 'Billie Jean' by Michael Jackson
5 'Brand New Key' by Melanie Safka
6 'Lucy In The Sky With Diamonds', from the Beatles' 'Sgt Pepper' LP
7 'The Lion Sleeps Tonight', which has been a number one for Tight Fit
8 'He'll Have To Stay'
9 'School Day'
10 'I'd Like To Buy The World A Coke'

 **B**

1 'Sloop John B'
2 'Clair de Lune'
3 'Je T'Aime . . . Moi Non Plus' by Serge Gainsbourg and Jane Birkin
4 'Remember Diana', a spin-off from 'Diana'
5 'I'm Still Dreaming', a spin-off from 'Dreaming'
6 'El Paso City', a spin-off from 'El Paso'
7 'Judy's Turn To Cry', a spin-off from 'It's My Party'
8 'Mandy' by Barry Manilow
9 'Mack The Knife' by Bobby Darin. It has also been a hit under the title 'Theme From The Threepenny Opera'
10 'Wooden Heart'

 **C**

1 'Pauvre Jean'
2 'Along Came Caroline', a spin-off from Angela Jones. The lyrics included the lines 'I used to sing of Angela, and then along came Caroline'.
3 'Can't Help Falling In Love'
4 'Lay Down Your Arms' by Anne Shelton
5 'Randy Scouse Git'
6 Dusty Springfield took 'You Don't Have To Say You Love Me' to number one.
7 'You're Having The Last Dance With Me'
8 It was originally recorded by Racey, as 'Kitty'
9 'YMCA' and 'In The Navy', both hits for Village People
10 'Congratulations' by Bill Martin and Phil Coulter, a number one for Cliff Richard in 1968

ANSWERS

QUIZ 26
GAYE

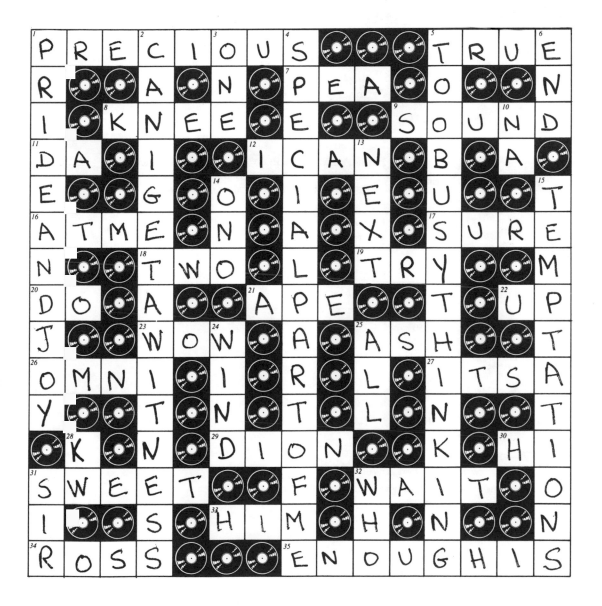

ANSWERS

QUIZ 27
WE DON'T TALK ANYMORE

 A

1 Shadows
2 Russ Conway
3 Champs
4 Simon Park Orchestra
5 Elton John
6 Shadows
7 Tornados
8 Shadows
9 B Bumble & The Stingers
10 Madness
11 Mike Oldfield
12 Lord Rockingham's XI
13 Vangelis
14 Meco
15 Fleetwood Mac

B

1 Ventures
2 Lieutenant Pigeon
3 Shadows
4 Ferrante & Teicher
5 Bill Justis
6 Duane Eddy
7 Russ Conway
8 Perez Prado and Eddie Calvert (both answers correct, double points for both names – the only instance of two versions of one instrumental hitting number one in the UK)
9 Horst Jankowski
10 Marcello Minerbi
11 The Rah Band
12 Focus
13 Royal Philharmonic Orchestra (conductor Louis Clark)
14 Ennio Morricone
15 Emerson, Lake & Palmer

 **C**

1 Johnny Winter's – Edgar
2 'Soul Limbo' by Booker T & the MGs
3 Geoff Love
4 Russ Conway and Winifred Atwell
5 a). It reached number 70 during a 9 week chart run in the States
6 The Allman Brothers Band
7 The Spotniks
8 Acker Bilk and Kenny Ball
9 'Stranger On The Shore' (Acker) and 'Midnight In Moscow' (Kenny). Bilk made number one, Kenny merely number two, both in 1962
10 Chris Barber, whose biggest single success, 'Petite Fleur', featured his clarinettist, Monty Sunshine, and not him
11 Space with 'Magic Fly'
12 'Flying'
13 'Liquidator'
14 'The Good The Bad And The Ugly' for Hugo Montenegro
15 The Simon Park Orchestra - 'Eye Level'

QUIZ 28
THE WORKER

1 The Silhouettes
2 Carpenters
3 The Merseybeats
4 Two Ton Ted from Teddington – he drove the baker's van
5 The Chain Gang
6 Car 23
7 Truck driver
8 Postman (he was the Singing Postman)
9 'The Chauffeur'
10 'Kaiser Bill's Batman' (on the other side he was Bizet's carman)

QUIZ 29
LIFE IS A LONG SONG

This is the complete story:

All the young dudes/ tell me to my face/ I'm the leader of the gang (I am). Nevertheless/ I'm not a juvenile delinquent/ but I do/ get tough/ when/ you drive me crazy. Why can't you/ love me like I love you? No doubt about it */ I go ape/ without you#. Last night */ I confess/ I shot the sherriff */ at the club/ just for kicks. Now */ Indiana wants me/ so here I am */ running scared. I could be happy/ somewhere */ they don't know/ me and my life. If only I could live my life again/ I'd do anything/ to be loved. I'm looking out the window/ watching the detectives/ looking for clues. I can see clearly now/ here comes the judge. Oh well */ I surrender. One fine day/ I shall be released.

The first letters of the asterisked clues were N L I N S S O, which can be rearranged to spell Nilsson, the man who took 'Without You' to number one.

ANSWERS

QUIZ 30
YEARS MAY COME, YEARS MAY GO

	A		B		C
1	1956	1	1979	1	1975
2	1969	2	1971	2	1960
3	1967	3	1964	3	1982
4	1976	4	1965	4	1980
5	1978	5	1964	5	1954
6	1952	6	1969	6	1962
7	1955	7	1979	7	1975
8	1959	8	1973	8	1955
9	1983	9	1975	9	1972
10	1977	10	1971	10	1965
11	1967	11	1968	11	1976
12	1970	12	1978	12	1967
13	1977	13	1977	13	1968
14	1973	14	1964	14	1956
15	1982	15	1970	15	1973
16	1980	16	1963	16	1968
17	1970	17	1953	17	1968
18	1970	18	1968	18	1960
19	1978	19	1979	19	1961
20	1968	20	1959	20	1954

QUIZ 31
CHAINS

1 Jack Bruce
2 Eric Clapton
3 Jeff Beck
4 Both Rod Stewart and Ron Wood
5 Tetsu Yamauchi
6 Both Simon Kirke and Paul Rodgers
7 Boz Burrel
8 John Wetton
9 David O'List
10 Keith Emerson
11 Carl Palmer
12 Chris Farlowe
13 Don Airey
14 Ritchie Blackmore
15 Harvey Hinsley

 **B**

1 They performed together on the number one single 'Xanadu'
2 Roy Wood and Bev Bevan played in both groups
3 The Move's single 'Flowers In The Rain' was the first record played on Radio 1. The group Brown Sauce was made up of Radio 1 disc jockeys and BBC TV presenters
4 Keith Chegwin and Maggie Philbin from Brown Sauce both work with Tony Blackburn on his Radio 1 weekend shows
5 Both artists recorded songs called 'It's Only Love' though they were different songs
6 Floyd played piano on many of Elvis' early hits
7 Both have had British number ones with instrumental discs
8 The Shadows were originally called the Drifters but changed their name because of the US group
9 The Drifters recorded a song called 'Save The Last Dance For Me', Engelbert had a number one with 'The Last Waltz'
10 Engelbert's first hit of the seventies was called 'My Marie', Shaky had a hit with 'Marie Marie'
11 Many of Shaky's hits were produced by Stuart Colman who used to be in Pinkerton's Assorted Colours
12 Both acts recorded songs called 'Mirror Mirror' though they were different songs
13 Dollar had a hit with a version of the Beatles' song 'I Want To Hold Your Hand'
14 Mick Jagger sang on the Beatles' record 'All You Need Is Love'
15 He was also guest vocalist on Peter Tosh's '(You Gotta Walk) Don't Look Back'
16 Peter Tosh recorded a reggae version of Berry's 'Johnny B Goode'
17 Both had hits with songs that repeated the same word three times in the title. 'Go Go Go' and 'Jam Jam Jam' respectively
18 Both recorded for the Philadelphia International label
19 The Three Degrees are said to be Prince Charles' favourite group and Duran Duran are said to be the favourite of Diana, Princess of Wales
20 Both made their Top 40 debut on 14 March 1981
21 Both recorded songs with "A-Go-Go" in the title, 'Einstein A-Go-Go' and 'Going To A-Go-Go'
22 The Beat covered Smokey's 'Tears Of A Clown'
23 Both had their first hit on the Two Tone label before moving elsewhere
24 Both recorded songs with the same name as the group
25 They recorded together as Headgirl
26 Girlschool covered Gun's hit 'Race With The Devil'
27 They both made their Top Ten debut in 18 December 1968
28 Dave Edmunds was guitarist with Love Sculpture
29 Both appeared in big rock films of the seventies, Edmunds in *Stardust* and Travolta in *Saturday Night Fever* and *Grease*
30 Olivia Newton John appeared with Travolta in *Grease* and had two number ones duets with him

ANSWERS

QUIZ 32
WHO AM I

 A

1 Blue Sky
2 Tambourine Man
3 Guitar
4 Zero
5 Crowley
6 Bass Man
7 Sandman
8 Raffles and Soft
9 Guder
10 President

QUIZ 33

LET THERE BE DRUMS

 A

1 Ringo Starr
2 Charlie Watts
3 Roger Taylor
4 Keith Moon
5 Roger Taylor
6 Bobby Elliott
7 Stewart Copeland
8 Dave Clark
9 Tony Meehan
10 Brian Bennett
11 Jerry Allison
12 Rick Buckler
13 Mick Fleetwood
14 Mitch Mitchell
15 D J Fontana
16 Bev Bevan
17 Bev Bevan
18 Jon Moss
19 Ginger Baker
20 Paul McCartney

 **B**

1 Clem Burke
2 Nigel Ollson
3 Freddie Marsden
4 Chris Curtis
5 Mick Avory
6 Mike Hugg
7 Jim McCarty
8 Pete York
9 Mick Wilson
10 Dave Munden
11 Hugh Grundy
12 Legs Larry Smith
13 Hal Blaine
14 Hal Blaine
15 Levon Helm
16 Doug Clifford
17 Jez Strode
18 Martin Chambers
19 John Steel
20 No drums!

 **C**

1 Bobby Gregg
2 Carl Palmer
3 Dennis Bryon
4 Earl Palmer
5 Mark Pinder
6 Roger Palm
7 Dennis Davis
8 Stuart Elliott
9 Jim Gordon
10 Clark Pierson
11 Jeff Porcaro
12 Ralph Jones
13 Murray Harmon
14 Brian Innes
15 Kenny Jones
16 Jim Keltner
17 Buddy Saltzman
18 Gerry Polci
19 Paul McCartney
20 Clem Cattini

QUIZ 34
CALL UP THE GROUPS

 A

1. Smurfs
2. Ants
3. Tijuana Brass
4. Drells
5. Holding Company
6. MGs
7. Attractions
8. Coconuts
9. Dinosaurs
10. Juniors
11. Aces
12. Dominos
13. Belmonts
14. Blockheads
15. Bunnymen
16. Mindbenders
17. Checkmates
18. Playboy Band
19. Pacemakers
20. Furious Five
21. Comets
22. Cockney Rebel
23. Crickets
24. Shondells
25. Blackhearts
26. Fish
27. Sunshine Band
28. Pirates
29. Pips
30. Gang
31. Dakotas
32. Teenagers
33. Papas
34. Wailers
35. Bluenotes
36. Rumour
37. Heartbreakers
38. Tremeloes
39. Union Gap
40. Vandellas
41. Modern Lovers
42. Miracles
43. First Edition
44. Supremes
45. Silver Bullet Band
46. Replays
47. Family Stone
48. Blue Jeans
49. Faces
50. All-Stars

B

1. Soul Sonic Force
2. Lost Trios Paranoias
3. Magic Band
4. Midnighters
5. Stingers
6. Sparkletones
7. Rebel Rousers
8. Tabulations
9. Crawlers
10. Lost Planet Airmen
11. Alphabeta
12. Wurzels
13. Evergreens
14. Starliters
15. Sex-O-Lettes
16. Trinity
17. Hotrods
18. Fentones
19. Gingerbreads
20. Vagabonds
21. Americans
22. Hurricanes
23. Bandwagon
24. Blue Belles
25. Band Slim Chance
26. Playboys
27. News
28. Family Cookin'
29. Dipsticks
30. Imperials
31. World's Famous Supreme Team
32. Music of the Mountains
33. Brasil '66
34. Enchanters (also accepted: Truckin' Co)
35. Crypt Kickers
36. Mysterians
37. Raiders
38. Romantics
39. Detroit Wheels
40. Pharaohs
41. B Devotion
42. Limelites
43. Beatles
44. Company
45. Our Gang
46. Blue Caps
47. Kinshasa Band
48. Ram Jam Band
49. Zodiacs
50. Afternoon Boys

C

1. Unitone
2. Hearts
3. Tuxedos
4. Bellboys
5. Forbidden
6. Love Squad
7. All-Night Newsboys
8. Rockets
9. Mighty Avons
10. Rhondels
11. Cast of Idiots
12. Don'ts
13. Heywoods
14. BBS Unlimited
15. Big Sound
16. Zigzag Jive Flutes
17. Fenmen
18. Continental Kids
19. Knockouts
20. Troopers
21. Easy Riders
22. FLO
23. Jaywalkers
24. Strange Behaviour
25. In-Men
26. Romans
27. Hand People
28. Citizen's Band
29. Greek Serenaders
30. Big Roll Band
31. Fabulous Twilights
32. Rhythm Aces
33. Big Apple Band
34. Invisible Girls
35. Gladiators
36. First National Band
37. Emblems
38. Jumping Jacks
39. Rainbows
40. Cottagers
41. Daytonas
42. Originals
43. Christmas Trees
44. Redheads
45. Mustafas
46. Radio Revellers
47. Hands of Dr Teleny
48. Sunglows
49. Dominos
50. Cavaliers

ANSWERS

QUIZ 35
WHAT HAVE THEY DONE TO MY SONG MA

 A

1 Ronettes, 'Baby I Love You'
2 Eddie Cochran, 'Summertime Blues'
3 Elvis Presley, 'Don't Be Cruel'
4 Robert Knight, 'Everlasting Love'
5 Little Richard, 'Good Golly Miss Molly'
6 Righteous Brothers, 'You've Lost That Loving Feeling'
7 Dionne Warwick, 'Walk On By'
8 Conway Twitty, 'It's Only Make Believe'
9 Rolling Stones, (I Can't Get No) 'Satisfaction'
10 Dusty Springfield, 'I Only Want To Be With You'
11 Inez and Charlie Foxx, 'Mockingbird'
12 Bill Haley and his Comets, 'Rock Around The Clock'
13 Zombies, 'She's Not There'
14 Neil Diamond, 'Red Red Wine'
15 Four Tops, 'It's The Same Old Song'

 B

1 Fats Domino, 'Ain't That A Shame'
2 Marv Johnson, 'You Got What It Takes'
3 Frankie Avalon, 'Why'
4 Smokey Robinson and the Miracles, 'Tracks Of My Tears'
5 Jerry Lee Lewis, 'Great Balls Of Fire'
6 Bob Marley, 'I Shot The Sheriff'
7 Eddie Floyd, 'Knock On Wood'
8 Chuck Berry, 'Memphis Tennessee' (Lonnie Mack's instrumental
      version was just called 'Memphis')
9 Sam Cooke, 'Bring It On Home To Me'
10 Shep and the Limelites, 'Daddy's Home'
11 Gene Vincent, 'Be Bop A Lula'
12 Little Richard, 'Rip It Up'
13 Jerry Lordan, 'Apache'
14 Jerry Keller, 'Here Comes Summer'
15 John Lennon, 'Imagine'

 C

1 Screaming Jay Hawkins, 'I Put A Spell On You'
2 Johnny Mathis, 'Twelfth Of Never'
3 Sonny James, 'Young Love'
4 Bob Dylan, 'All Along The Watchtower'
5 Nat King Cole, 'Nature Boy'
6 Bob Dylan, 'I Shall Be Released'
7 Doors, 'Light My Fire'
8 Kinks, 'I Go To Sleep'
9 Troggs, 'I Can't Control Myself'

10   Roy Orbison, 'Crying'
11   Serge Gainsbourg and Jane Birkin, 'Je T'aime . . . Moi Non Plus'
12   Valentinos, 'It's All Over Now'
13   Yazoo, 'Only You'
14   Leslie Gore, 'It's My Party'
15   Iggy Pop, 'Nightclubbing'

QUIZ 36
PICTURE THIS

1   Michael Holliday
2   Ronnie Hilton
3   Mel Torme
4   Tab Hunter
5   Billy Eckstine
6   Eddie Fisher
7   David Whitfield
8   Dean Martin (*left*) who had 17 hits and his comedy partner Jerry Lewis
9   Frankie Vaughan
10   Terry Dene

QUIZ 37
KING CREOLE

1   *Jailhouse Rock*
2   *King Creole*, based on 'A Stone For Danny Fisher'
3   *G I Blues*
4   *Blue Hawaii*
5   *Kissin' Cousins*
6   *Speedway*
7   *G I Blues*. Juliet Prowse was at one time engaged to Frank Sinatra
8   *Blue Hawaii*
9   *Love Me Tender*
10   *Elvis: That's The Way It Is*

ANSWERS

 B

1 *King Creole*
2 *Kid Galahad*
3 *Tickle Me*
4 Shelley Fabares, whose 'Johnny Angel' hit number one. Her first Elvis movie was *Girl Happy*.
5 *Live A Little Love A Little*
6 *G I Blues*
7 *Fun In Acapulco*, director Richard Thorpe
8 *Change Of Habit*
9 *Love Me Tender*, producer David Weisbart
10 *It Happened At The World's Fair*

 C

1 *Kid Galahad*. Michael Curtiz had directed both the 1937 version and *King Creole* 21 years later
2 *Girls Girls Girls*, script by Edward Anhalt
3 *Roustabout*
4 *Jailhouse Rock*
5 *King Creole*
6 Ann-Margret co-starred in *Love in Las Vegas*. Her film with Art Garfunkel was *Carnal Knowledge*. Her Top 20 hit was 'I Just Don't Understand' which reached number 17 in the autumn of 1961.
7 *Tickle Me*
8 *Frankie and Johnny*
9 *Spinout*. The track is 'Tomorrow Is A Long Time'.
10 *King Creole*

QUIZ 38
WHAT'D I SAY

A

1 'One Step Beyond', Madness, Melodisc Music Ltd
2 '(Just Like) Starting Over', John Lennon, Lenono Music/Warner Brothers Music
3 'Rocket Man', Elton John, Dick James Music
4 'Rock Around the Clock', Bill Haley and his Comets, Myers
5 'Eleanor Rigby', Beatles, Northern Songs
6 'American Pie', Don McLean, Intersong Music Ltd
7 'Blue Suede Shoes', Carl Perkins, Hill and Range/Hi-Lo
8 'Bohemian Rhapsody', Queen, Trident Music
9 'The Onion Song', Marvin Gaye and Tammi Terrell, Jobete-London Ltd
10 'Let's Twist Again', Chubby Checker, Carlin Music

11 'Leader of the Pack', Shangri-Las, Robert Mellin Ltd
12 'Modern Love', David Bowie, Jones Music
13 'Do You Want To Know A Secret?', Beatles, Northern Songs
14 'Do You Really Want To Hurt Me?', Culture Club, Virgin Music
15 'Happy Xmas (War Is Over)', John and Yoko/Plastic Ono Band with the
      Harlem Community Choir, Ono Music/ATV Music

 **B**

1 'San Franciscan Nights', Eric Burdon, A. Schroeder Music/Slamina
2 'Patches', Clarence Carter, Gold Forever Music
3 'Bye Bye Baby', Bay City Rollers, Ardmore and Beechwood Ltd
4 'Tell Laura I Love Her', Ray Peterson, Lawrence Wright Music Co. Ltd
5 'Can't Get Enough Of Your Love Babe', Barry White, Interworld Music
      Ltd
6 'Take Good Care Of My Baby', Bobby Vee, Aldon Music
7 'Speedy Gonzales', Pat Boone, Budd Music-Mecolico BIEM
8 'Here There And Everywhere', Beatles, Northern Songs
9 'Runaround Sue', Dion, Rust Enterprises
10 'I Left My Heart In San Francisco', Tony Bennett, Dash Music
11 'Soldier Boy', Shirelles, ABKCO/Ludix
12 'Ruby Tuesday', Rolling Stones, Mirage Music
13 'Ain't No Mountain High Enough', Diana Ross, Jobete-Carlin Music Ltd
14 'In Dreams', Roy Orbison, Acuff-Rose Music Ltd
15 'Hats Off To Larry', Del Shannon, MAJ Music

 **C**

1 'Do You Love Me?', Contours, Dominion Music Ltd
2 'Fingertips Pt 2', Stevie Wonder, Jobete Music Co Inc/Stone Agate
      Music Division
3 'Only The Strong Survive', Jerry Butler, Downstairs Music/Double
      Diamond Music/Parabut Music
4 'Sixteen Candles', Coronation Music/January Music
5 'Stagger Lee', Lloyd Price, United Artists Music
6 'Uptown', Crystals, Columbia/Screen Gems
7 'See You In September', Tempos, Vibar Music
8 'Shoop Shoop Song', Betty Everett, T M Music
9 'Walkin' In The Rain With The One I Love', Love Unlimited, Interworld
      Music Ltd
10 'W.O.L.D.', Harry Chapin, Story Songs Ltd
11 'Take A Message To Mary', Everly Brothers, Acuff-Rose Music
12 'Folsom Prison Blues' (1968 live version), Johnny Cash, Carlin Music
13 'Dear Lady Twist', Gary "US" Bonds, Dizzy Heights Music Pub
      Ltd/Rockmasters Ltd
14 'When My Little Girl Is Smiling', Drifters, Screen Gems/Columbia
15 'Hit Record', Brook Benton, Luristan Music, Dave Dreyer Music, and
      Dayben Music

ANSWERS

QUIZ 39
LOOKING AFTER NUMBER ONE

 A

1 'Can The Can' by Suzi Quatro
2 The Electric Light Orchestra, though they did have a number one in
    collaboration with Olivia Newton John
3 'The Israelites' by Desmond Dekker and the Aces
4 Frank Sinatra waited 11 years 244 days between his two number
    ones, 'Three Coins In A Fountain' and 'Strangers In The Night'
5 'Here In My Heart' by Al Martino. The first chart was published on 14
    November 1952.
6 'Get Back'
7 'Jealous Guy'
8 'Surrender'
9 (Scott) Engel, (John) Maus and (Gary) Leeds
10 Vincent Van Gogh in Don McLean's 'Vincent' and L S Lowry in Brian
    Michael's 'Matchstalk Men And Matchstalk Cats And Dogs'
11 'Bright Eyes' by Art Garfunkel was written by Mike Batt, the man behind the Wombles
12 'Pipes Of Peace' by Paul McCartney
13 'Two Little Boys' by Rolf Harris
14 Theme From M.A.S.H (Suicide Is Painless)
15 Gerry and the Pacemakers

 B

1 'Lady Madonna'
2 'Cathy's Clown' by the Everly Brothers. It was the first UK release for
    the label.
3 'Coz I Luv You' by Slade
4 'Honky Tonk Women'
5 Stig Anderrson received credit as co-writer on the first six but only
    Benny and Bjorn were credited on the last three
6 Art Garfunkel, 'I Only Have Eyes For You' and 'Bright Eyes'
7 'What Do You Want To Make Those Eyes At Me For?' by Emile Ford
    and the Checkmates followed 'What Do You Want' by Adam Faith
8 Mungo Jerry
9 Billy J Kramer and the Dakotas, Peter and Gordon, Overlanders, Joe
    Cocker and Marmalade
10 The Shadows with 'Foot Tapper'
11 Dave Gilmour
12 Kris Kristofferson
13 'In The Year 2525' by Zager and Evans
14 'Sugar Sugar' by the Archies
15 'Mr Tambourine Man' and 'Mighty Quinn'

 **C**

1 Paul Anka
2 Sandie Shaw

3 Russ Ballard wrote the former and played guitar on the latter
4 'Wooden Heart' by Elvis Presley
5 Tammy Wynette
6 'Do Ya Think I'm Sexy' by Rod Stewart
7 The Poppy Family
8 Milt Gabler
9 The Four Preps
10 Terry Melcher, son of Doris Day
11 'Carousel', Shirley Jones
12 'Forget Me Not'
13 Four Seasons
14 Baccara
15 The first was 'Moulin Rouge' by Mantovani and the last 'Eye Level' by
     the Simon Park Orchestra

QUIZ 40
I GET AROUND

1 Rowboat
2 Trains/Boats/Planes
3 Pushbike
4 Honda
5 Cadillac
6 Train
7 Jet Airliner
8 Combine Harvester
9 Jet Plane
10 Bicycle

QUIZ 41
HERE THERE AND EVERYWHERE

1 Waterloo
2 Argentina, 'Don't Cry For Me Argentina'
3 San Francisco
4 Massachusetts
5 Chicago
6 Babylon, 'Rivers Of Babylon'
7 Mull Of Kintyre
8 Penny Lane
9 California Girls
10 London, 'Streets Of London'
11 Baker Street
12 Mercury, Freddie Mercury
13 Venus, 'Venus In Blue Jeans'
14 Earth, 'Planet Earth'
15 Phoenix, 'By The Time I Get To Phoenix'
16 Moon, 'The Dark Side Of The Moon'
17 Dover, 'White Cliffs Of Dover'
18 Liverpool, 'Long Haired Lover From Liverpool'
19 Durham, 'Durham Town (The Leavin')'
20 Japan

ANSWERS

 **B**

1   Tahiti
2   Georgia, 'Georgia On My Mind'
3   France, 'Lost In France'
4   Cumberland Gap
5   San José, 'Do You Know The Way To San José'
6   Cambodia
7   Zambesi
8   San Fernando, 'Last Train To San Fernando'
9   Clarksville, 'Last Train To Clarksville'
10 Paris, 'Paris Match'
11 Xanadu, 'Legend Of Xanadu'
12 Memphis, Tennessee
13 Carolina, 'Carolina Moon'
14 Kentucky, 'Blue Moon Of Kentucky'
15 Wardour Street, ' "A" Bomb In Wardour Street'
16 Bermuda, 'Bermuda Triangle'
17 Tucson, Arizona, 'Get Back'
18 Mississippi
19 Woodstock
20 New York, 'The Only Living Boy In New York'

C

1   Finchley Central
2   Bowling Green
3   Washington and Oregon ("Now in Washington and Oregon you can hear the factories hum"), 'Grand Coulee Dam' by Lonnie Donegan
4   Spanish Harlem
5   Spain, 'Never Been To Spain'
6   Frankfurt, 'Frankfurt Special', from *G I Blues*
7   New Jersey, 'Delaware', by Perry Como,
    ("What did Della wear, boys?
    She wore a brand New Jersey")
8   Navarone, 'Guns Of Navarone', from 'Special A K A Live' EP
9   Scarborough, 'Scarborough Fair'
10 Los Angeles, 'Comin' In To Los Angeles', by Arlo Guthrie
11 New Orleans, 'City Of New Orleans', 'Walkin' To New Orleans'
12 Jamaica, 'Jamaica, Say You Will'
13 France, 'Tour de France'
14 Istanbul
15 Asia Minor
16 Canterbury
17 Kinshasa, the Kinshasa Band backed Johnny Wakelin on 'In Zaire'
18 Omaha, from 'Kansas City Star' by Roger Miller
19 Bangor, Maine, from 'King Of The Road' by Roger Miller
20 Albuquerque, from 'Promised Land' by Chuck Berry

QUIZ 42

I'M GONNA SIT RIGHT DOWN AND WRITE MYSELF A LETTER

A   Paul Simon, Art Garfunkel
B   Bookends
C   OK?
D   Chicago
E   Bridge Over, Water
F   I See
G   Midget
H   Dr Hook
I   Say Say
J   Mamma Mia
K   I Die
L   I Am A Rock

M   Hi
N   The Race Is On
O   Dot
P   Without
Q   Thyme
R   Soft
S   Wife
T   On

From 'America', copyright Paul Simon.

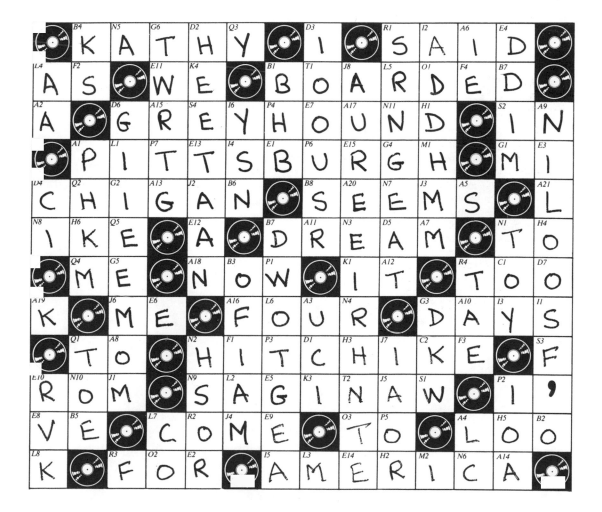

ANSWERS

QUIZ 43
THE SHOW MUST GO ON

 A

1 *Cats* – Elaine Paige
2 *My Fair Lady* – Vic Damone
3 *Evita* – Linda Lewis
4 *West Side Story* – P J Proby
5 *A Little Night Music* – Judy Collins
6 *Pyjama Game* – Johnston Brothers
7 *Hair* – Oliver
8 *Oliver* – Shirley Bassey
9 *Godspell* – Holly Sherwood
10 *Mr Cinders* – Sting
11 *Me And Juliet* – Ronnie Hilton
12 *Funny Girl* – Tymes
13 *South Pacific* – Captain Sensible
14 *Kismet* – Tony Bennett
15 *Aladdin* – Shadows

 B

1 *Grease* – John Travolta & Olivia Newton-John
2 *Fame* – Irene Cara
3 *The Poseidon Adventure* – Maureen McGovern
4 *The Young Ones* – Cliff Richard
5 *Blue Hawaii* – Elvis Presley
6 *The Rose* – Bette Midler
7 *Rocky III* – Survivor
8 *The Spy Who Loved Me* – Carly Simon
9 *Silver Dream Racer* – David Essex
10 *American Gigolo* – Blondie
11 *A Star Is Born* – Barbra Streisand
12 *Saturday Night Fever* – Bee Gees
13 *Octopussy* – Rita Coolidge
14 *You Light Up My Life* – Debbie Boone
15 *Three Coins In The Fountain* – Frank Sinatra

 C

1 *Saturday Night Fever*
2 *ABBA – The Movie*
3 (a) *King Creole* (b) *Blue Hawaii* (c) *Loving You* (d) *Fun In Acapulco*
4 Isaac Hayes
5 (a) Marti Webb (b) *Tell Me On A Sunday* (c) 'Take That Look Off Your Face' (d) *Song And Dance*
6 'Tubular Bells' – Mike Oldfield
7 Play It Cool
8 *Hair*
9 *Jesus Christ Superstar*
10 *Deliverance* – Duelling Banjos
11 Jennifer Holliday
12 *Paint Your Wagon*
13 Moulin Rouge – Mantovani
14 (a) *Live And Let Die* (b) *The Spy Who Loved Me* (c) *From Russia With Love*
15 *South Pacific*, 1959

QUIZ 44
SOLDIER BOY

 A

1 Hollies
2 'I Don't Wanna Be A Soldier' by John Lennon
3 Anne Shelton – 'Lay Down Your Arms'
4 The Stranglers
5 Mungo Jerry
6 Staff Sergeant
7 Generals and Majors
8 'The Dambusters March', Central Band of the Royal Air Force
9 The Damned
10 Andy Stewart

ANSWERS

QUIZ 45
MY NAME IS JACK

A

1 Paul and Arthur
2 Daryl and John
3 Richard and Marvin
4 Sinatra and Hazlewood
5 Lennon and Ono
6 Duran Duran
7 Depeche Mode
8 Abba
9 Buck's Fizz
10 Beatles
11 Ringo Starr
12 Cliff Richard
13 David Bowie
14 Boy George
15 Sting
16 Lulu
17 Engelbert Humperdinck
18 Elton John
19 Cilla Black
20 Buddy Holly
21 Tommy Steele
22 Gary Numan
23 Tennessee Ernie Ford
24 Doris Day
25 Bob Dylan

B

1 David and Ryuichi
2 Kevin and Lol
3 Berry and Torrence
4 Asher and Waller
5 Bono
6 Mungo Jerry
7 UB40
8 Tremeloes
9 Temperance Seven
10 Dire Straits
11 Dusty Springfield
12 Tom Jones
13 Georgie Fame
14 Adam Faith
15 The Big Bopper
16 Mike McGear
17 Eden Kane
18 Gary Glitter (a half mark for Paul Raven)
19 John Denver
20 Alice Cooper
21 Russ Conway
22 Marc Bolan
23 Aneka
24 Brian and Michael
25 Tammy Wynette

ANSWERS

 C

1 Tom and Hughie
2 Denny and Rick
3 Peretti and Creatore
4 Forest and Reid
5 Seville – this 'duo' was actually David Seville playing two parts. For David Seville's real name, see 15
6 Searchers
7 Alice Cooper
8 Union Gap
9 Mindbenders
10 Three Dog Night
11 Typically Tropical
12 Billy Fury
13 Craig Douglas
14 P J Proby
15 David Seville, Alfi and Harry, or the Chipmunks. He was all of them
16 Sandie Shaw
17 Paul Jones
18 Billy J Kramer
19 Del Shannon
20 Bobby Darin
21 Ricky Valance
22 Conway Twitty
23 Frankie Laine
24 Dean Martin
25 Alvin Stardust or Shane Fenton

QUIZ 46
WORDY RAPPINGHOOD

 A   B   C

	A	B	C
1	Oak	Cheerful	Harmonica
2	Baby	Hop	Noise
3	Love	Zoo	Day-Glo
4	Hand	Run	Neck
5	UK	Dustpipe	Yours
6	Moon	Send	Forever
7	Brick	Swing	Booty
8	Love	Drop	River
9	Woman	Fourth	Sighs
10	Doggie	Guest	Bully
11	Wine	Tulsa	17
12	Star	Ah	Baby
13	Me	World	Bells
14	Love	Me	Band
15	Ivory	Casbah	Birds
16	Shakin'	Sixteen	Lovelight
17	Deliver	Earth	Light
18	Fun	Can	Drum
19	Sun	Night	Wings
20	Grapevine	You	Letter

ANSWERS

QUIZ 47
LOOKING FOR CLUES

1   Beatles
2   Tom Jones
3   Rod Stewart
4   10CC
5   Roy Orbison
6   Donny Osmond
7   Foreigner
8   Del Shannon
9   Alan Price
10 Rolling Stones
11 Clash
12 Roy Wood
13 Stevie Wonder
14 Kinks
15 Midge Ure
16 Mott The Hoople
17 Rolf Harris
18 Philip Lynott
19 Cliff Richard
20 Smokey/Smokie

QUIZ 48
OH WHAT A CIRCUS

1   From the musical *Evita*
2   Dave Davies, 'Death Of A Clown'
3   Linda Carr and the Love Squad
4   One The Juggler
5   Big Top
6   Mr Kite's, The Beatles' 'Being For The Benefit Of Mr Kite'
7   Henry the Horse
8   Pat Boone in 1962
9   Micky Dolenz of the Monkees
10 Elton John in 'Little Jeannie'

QUIZ 49
FIRST CUT IS THE DEEPEST

1   'Love Me Do'
2   'It's Not Unusual'
3   'Waterloo'
4   'Apache'
5   'Planet Earth'
6   'Do You Want To Know A Secret?'
7   'Seven Seas Of Rhye'
8   'Another Day'
9   'Kings Of The Wild Frontier'
10 'Ne Ne Na Na Nu Nu'
11 'Making Your Mind Up'
12 'Do You Really Want To Hurt Me?'
13 'In The Summertime'
14 'Begin the Beguine (Volver A Empezar)'
15 'First Cut Is The Deepest'
16 'Go Now'
17 'Are "Friends" Electric?'
18 'The Wombling Song'
19 'You've Lost That Lovin' Feelin''
20 'Sherry'
21 Elvis Presley
22 David Bowie
23 Soft Cell
24 Elton John
25 Sex Pistols
26 Roy Orbison
27 Cliff Richard
28 Roxy Music
29 Don McLean
30 Madness
31 Blondie
32 Elvis Costello
33 Dr Hook
34 Connie Francis
35 Engelbert Humperdinck
36 Jam
37 Jonathan King
38 Nicole
39 Donna Summer
40 Police

ANSWERS

 B

1 'Baby Let Me Take You Home'
2 'Love Of The Loved'
3 'No Woman No Cry'
4 'Love Is Life'
5 'Surfin' USA'
6 'Queen Of Clubs'
7 '10538 Overture'
8 'The Show Must Go On'
9 'School Day'
10 'If Not For You'
11 'Dead Pop Stars'
12 'Charmaine'
13 'New York Mining Disaster' 1941
14 'Pearl's A Singer'
15 'Do You Love Me?'
16 'Marjorine'
17 'The Times They Are A-Changing'
18 'Rock On'
19 'Peggy Sue'
20 'Holiday 80 (double single)'
21 Rolling Stones
22 Kingston Trio
23 Showaddywaddy
24 Helen Shapiro
25 Pretenders
26 Johnny Kidd & the Pirates
27 Modern Romance
28 Diana Ross
29 P J Proby
30 Status Quo
31 Bay City Rollers
32 Boney M
33 Darts
34 Joe Brown
35 Shakin' Stevens
36 Chicago
37 Sam Cooke
38 Cream
39 Dave Dee, Dozy, Beaky, Mick & Tich
40 Fleetwood Mac

 C

1 'Banana Boat Song'
2 Never had a hit single in UK!
3 'Homeward Bound'
4 'Young At Heart'
5 'Take Me I'm Yours'
6 'Second Hand Rose'
7 'Think'
8 'Enjoy Yourself'
9 'A Hard Rain's Gonna Fall'
10 'Lucky Devil'
11 'Supership'
12 'Wichita Lineman'
13 'Georgia On My Mind'
14 '007'
15 'Shooting Star'
16 'How Sweet It Is'
17 'I Know What I Like (In Your Wardrobe)'
18 'Just Like Me'
19 'Gentlemen Take Polaroids'
20 'Teacher Teacher'
21 Acker Bilk
22 Brotherhood Of Man
23 Petula Clark
24 Duane Eddy
25 Billy Fury
26 Mud
27 Johnny Nash
28 Nina and Frederick
29 XTC
30 Yardbirds
31 Coasters
32 Bill Haley
33 Dexy's Midnight Runners
34 Iron Maiden
35 Fats Domino
36 Dion
37 Rockey Sharpe & The Replays
38 Frankie Vaughan
39 Jimmy Young
40 Earth Wind and Fire

QUIZ 50
DETROIT CITY

 A

1 Smokey Robinson
2 Thelma Houston
3 Stevie Wonder
4 Rod Stewart, 'This Old Heart of Mine'
5 Martin Luther King
6 Saxophone (tenor sax, to be precise)
7 Marvin Gaye
8 R Dean Taylor
9 'Please Mr Postman'
10 'I'm Still Waiting'
11 'Abraham, Martin and John'
12 'What Becomes of the Brokenhearted'
13 'The Onion Song'
14 The Mary Jane Girls, 'All Night Long'
15 David Ruffin, the Temptations
16 Syreeta
17 'Being With You'
18 'Never Can Say Goodbye'
19 Levi Stubbs
20 'War'
21 'Truly'
22 Billy Preston
23 'One Day In Your Life'
24 'Love Machine'
25 'Machine Gun'

 B

1 Marvin Gaye and Tammi Terrell
2 'Up The Ladder To The Roof'
3 'What's Going On'
4 'Money', Barrett Strong
5 Ike and Tina Turner
6 Charlene
7 'I'm Living In Shame'
8 Rare Earth
9 'Beechwood 4-5789'
10 The Temptations
11 Jean Terrell
12 'Got To Be There'
13 'Shop Around'
14 'You Are The Sunshine Of My Life'
15 Kris Kristofferson
16 Brian, Lamont, and Eddie
17 'Ball Of Confusion'
18 'Talking Book'
19 'Tears of a Clown'
20 Marvin Gaye
21 Kiki Dee
22 *Mahogany*
23 'Standing In The Shadows Of Love'
24 Brenda Holloway
25 The Miracles

 C

1 'Urgent'
2 'Just My Soul Responding' by Smokey Robinson
3 'Two Lovers'
4 'You + Me = Love'
5 'Boogie Down'
6 'Reach Out I'll Be There' ('Baby Love' was a number one, but it was issued on the Stateside label)
7 'Indiana Wants Me' by R Dean Taylor
8 'You've Really Got A Hold On Me'
9 'How Sweet It Is'
10 Renaldo Benson of the Four Tops
11 Gordy
12 *Trouble Man*

13 The Four Seasons ('Night')
14 'Temptations With A Lot Of Soul'
15 Tom Clay
16 Eddie Holland
17 The Contours
18 'Once Upon A Time'
19 'Four Tops Live!'
20 Shorty Long
21 The Pips
22 'The Happening'
23 'These Things Will Keep Me Loving You'
24 'You Haven't Done Nothin''
25 Flyweight

ANSWERS

QUIZ 51
LABELLED WITH LOVE

 A

1 Parlophone
2 London-American
3 Tamla Motown
4 Epic
5 MCA
6 CBS
7 EMI
8 A & M
9 RCA
10 Mercury
11 Virgin
12 HMV
13 Decca
14 Regal-Zonophone
15 DJM

 B

1 Love Affair. The others hit on Decca
2 Lulu. All four hit on Polydor but the other three also hit on RCA
3 Cilla Black. The others hit on Columbia
4 Everly Brothers. The others hit on Polydor
5 Chelsea FC. The others hit on Chelsea
6 Julie Covington. The others hit on Polydor. (So did Julie but only as one of the Rock Follies female vocal quartet)
7 Bad Manners. The others hit on Stiff
8 Barry White. The others hit on Philadelphia International
9 Bananarama. The others hit on Chrysalis
10 Sweet. The others hit on RAK
11 B A Robertson. The others hit on Swansong
12 Pioneers. The others hit on Island
13 Brian Poole & The Tremeloes. The others hit on CBS
14 Phil Collins. The others hit on Charisma
15 Joy Division. The others hit on RCA

 C

1 A is for Alpert (Herb Alpert) and M is for Moss (Jerry Moss), co-founders of the label
2 Columbia
3 Lulu – Decca, Columbia, Atco, Polydor, Chelsea and Alfa. Her many appearances in part 2 of this section should have made this an easy one
4 'Je T'Aime . . . Moi Non Plus' by Jane Birkin and Serge Gainsbourg, from Fontana to Major Minor
5 Echo and the Bunnymen
6 T for Tamla, M for Motown, G for Gordy. (The three principal US labels owned by Berry Gordy)
7 St Winifred's School Choir (with 'There's No-one Quite Like Grandma')
8 The Who
9 Warner Brothers with 'Cathy's Clown' by the Everly Brothers
10 Page One and Penny Farthing
11 Triumph
12 (a) Brother (b) Swansong (C) Riva (d) Reprise (e) Rocket
13 Typically Tropical were on Gull Records
14 Philadelphia International, the only label not to have hit the UK charts with a release of 'Leader Of The Pack' by the Shangri-Las
15 Wayne Fontana. The label was of course Fontana (not Wayne)

QUIZ 52
THE ZOO

1 Simon and Garfunkel
2 Elephants
3 Pixilated
4 Mud with 'Tiger Feet'
5 Rhinoceros
6 Crocodile
7 British Lions
8 The Bonzo Dog Doo Dah Band in 'The Canyons Of Your Mind'
9 Rolf Harris in 'Tie Me Kangaroo Down Sport'
10 Rocky Raccoon

QUIZ 53
WHO CAN IT BE NOW?

A

1 Beatles
2 Adam & the Ants
3 Rolling Stones
4 Supremes
5 Shadows
6 Monkees
7 Animals
8 Kinks
9 Hollies
10 Dawn
11 Crickets
12 Searchers
13 Walker Brothers
14 Peter Green's Fleetwood Mac
15 Gerry & the Pacemakers

B

1 Doors
2 Band
3 Eurythmics
4 Lovin' Spoonful
5 Love
6 Manhattan Transfer
7 Soft Cell
8 Fifth Dimension
9 Squeeze
10 Three Dog Night
11 Scaffold
12 Cockney Rebel
13 Boston
14 Blood Sweat and Tears
15 Four Tops

C

1 Attractions
2 Herman's Hermits
3 Shirelles
4 Thunderclap Newman
5 Easybeats
6 Stylistics
7 Toto
8 Buffalo Springfield
9 Tymes
10 Tremeloes
11 Swinging Blue Jeans
12 Goombay Dance Band
13 Dr Hook
14 Showaddywaddy
15 Real Thing

QUIZ 54
BITS AND PIECES

1 (*left to right*) Eric Burdon, Otis Redding, Chris Farlowe
2 It is the street in Liverpool where the Cavern Club was situated
3 2 I's coffee bar in London's Old Compton Street, the home of the early British rock 'n roll and the starting point for artists like Cliff Richard, The Shadows, Tommy Steele and Adam Faith
4 (*left to right*) Ron, Stig, Dirk, Barry
5 Dave Edmunds (once) Noddy Holder of Slade (6 times) Les Gray of Mud (3 times)
6 Fabian
7 Percy Sledge
8 Joe Tex
9 Twinkle
10 Cliff Bennett

ANSWERS

QUIZ 55
WHO'S GONNA ROCK YOU

 A

 B

 C

	A	B	C
1	Guitar	Piano	Saxophone
2	Piano	Bass	Bass
3	Guitar	Drums	Saxophone
4	Drums	Piano	Keyboards
5	Piano	Guitar	Guitar
6	Bass	Trumpet	Banjo
7	Guitar	Drums	Piano
8	Guitar	Guitar	Guitar
9	Clarinet	Keyboards	Keyboards
10	Guitar	Piano	Organ
11	Guitar	Guitar	Saxophone
12	Trumpet	Piano	Drums
13	Bass	Saxophone	Trumpet
14	Keyboards	Guitar	Guitar
15	Trumpet	Keyboards	Piano
16	Guitar	Trombone	Organ
17	Keyboards	Drums	Clarinet
18	Drums	Saxophone	Guitar
19	Piano	Synthesisers	Keyboards
20	Guitar	Ukelele	Drums
21	Guitar	Drums	Keyboards
22	Guitar	Bass	Guitar
23	Synthesisers	Bass	Drums
24	Trombone	Keyboards	Organ
25	Piano	Pipes	Trumpet
26	Bass	Guitar	Guitar
27	Piano	Drums	Piano
28	Clarinet	Piano	Guitar
29	Piano	Trumpet	Organ
30	Drums	Piano	Bass
31	Guitar	Synthesisers	Guitar
32	Drums	Bass	Keyboards
33	Bass	Drums	Drums
34	Drums	Guitar	Piano
35	(Tenor) Saxophone	Trumpet	Flute
36	Drums	Guitar	Keyboards
37	Synthesisers	Harp	Bass
38	Guitar	Guitar	Drums
39	Piano	Trumpet	Guitar
40	Saxophone	Guitar	Bass
41	Guitar	Saxophone	Bass
42	Piano	Bass	Guitar
43	Guitar	Piano	Guitar
44	Guitar	Guitar	Bass
45	Piano	Piano	Drums
46	Flute	Drums	Keyboards
47	Guitar	Piano	Guitar
48	Guitar	Bass	Bass
49	Drums	Guitar	Guitar
50	Guitar	Trumpet	Keyboards

ANSWERS

51	Guitar	51	Synthesisers	51	Guitar
52	Bass	52	Guitar	52	Guitar
53	Guitar	53	Keyboards	53	Drums
54	Guitar	54	Drums	54	Guitar
55	Trumpet	55	Harmonica	55	Drums
56	Guitar	56	Guitar	56	Drums
57	Guitar	57	Piano	57	Drums (and Kawlimba)
58	Drums	58	Guitar	58	Bass
59	Bass	59	Saxophone	59	Keyboards
60	Guitar			60	Keyboards

QUIZ 56
ONE NATION UNDER A GROOVE

 **A**

1 Swedish
2 German
3 Dutch
4 German
5 Spanish
6 French
7 Australian
8 South African
9 Israeli
10 Spanish/German (bonus point for getting the German connection)
11 Japanese
12 Australian
13 Swedish
14 French
15 Greek

 **B**

1 Australian
2 Australian (Flash and the Pan and the Easybeats are both the brain children of top Aussie writer/producers Vanda and Young)
3 Spanish (she beat Cliff at Eurovision 1968)
4 Jamaican
5 French
6 Japanese
7 Jamaican
8 German
9 Dutch
10 French (though she won Eurovision for Monaco)
11 Dutch
12 Romanian
13 Dutch
14 New Zealander
15 Spanish

ANSWERS

 C

1 Anni-Frid Lyngstad (Frida)
2 Norway
3 Father Abraham and the Smurfs (from Holland)
4 Baccara
5 Julio Iglesias
6 Split Enz (from New Zealand)
7 In the Black Forest – in 1965. Like the Forest, Horst is German
8 Jean-Michel Jarre
9 Equinoxe (Part V)
10 Both had a hit with a song called 'Substitute' – but the Who's classic was not the song recorded by Clout for their only UK success
11 The Seekers and Paul Anka, from Australia and Canada respectively
12 Boney M. The song was 'Rivers Of Babylon' and it was recorded in Germany
13 They all won the Eurovision Song Contest
14 Lys Assia – hers was the only winner of the five not to have made the UK charts
15 Herbert Kretzmer, the distinguished British lyricist, wrote the words to Aznavour's number one 'She' and also to the Sellers/Loren biggie 'Goodness Gracious Me'

QUIZ 57
GARDEN OF EDEN

 A

1 Tiny Tim
2 Lynn Anderson
3 Eden Kane
4 'Ace Of Spades'
5 The grass grow
6 Lawn chairs
7 Genesis in 'I Know What I Like In Your Wardrobe'
8 The Seeds
9 Jethro Tull
10 Heinz, 'Diggin' My Potatoes'

QUIZ 58

STUCK IN THE MIDDLE WITH YOU

 A

1 Bill Wyman, the only non-Beatle
2 Billy Fury; the other two are the same man
3 Bobby Vee did not die in that Iowa plane crash in 1959
4 'Living Doll' by Cliff Richard, the others are by Elvis Presley
5 'Kissing To Be Clever' by Culture Club, the others are by the Police
6 *The Young Ones* starred Cliff Richard, the others were Elvis Presley films
7 Yellow Magic Orchestra. They are Japanese, the others are German
8 'Aladdin Sane'; the others were number one hit singles *and* albums
9 'Portsmouth', the only non-Tube station title
10 'Does Your Mother Know', the only one that was not number one for Abba (also the only one with a male lead vocal)

 B

1 Peter Fenton; the other two are the same man
2 Decca; the others are or were EMI labels
3 Kraftwerk; the others have had number one hits written by Neil Diamond
4 Lee Marvin; the others have had number one hits written by Rodgers and Hammerstein
5 Dollar, who are not brother and sister
6 Walker Brothers; the other groups all contain twins
7 Wings; the other groups all contain somebody called Maurice (Maurice Gibb, Maurice White and Maurice Williams)
8 Elvis; the others are all first names of hitmaking Williamses
9 Slade; the other groups all featured Roy Wood at some time
10 Donna Summer. Not only is she the only female, she is the only one who has not made a hit duet with Olivia Newton-John

 **C**

1 Ian Dury; the others are from noble families
2 Bob Dylan has not had a British hit single called 'Guilty'
3 Benny Hill did not have a hit with 'Volare'
4 Des O'Connor; his first hit single was not from a TV show
5 Ringo Starr was born on 7 July, the others on 17 Feb
6 'Japanese Boy' by Aneka did not feature Gary Tibbs on bass
7 Aneka did not win the Eurovision Song Contest
8 'If You Leave Me Now'; the others have all been hits in both vocal and instrumental versions
9 Ronnie Hilton. The others all have hitmaking daughters
10 Gene Pitney. He is the only one who has never had a hit single with a Lennon/McCartney song

I'M GONNA SIT RIGHT DOWN AND WRITE MYSELF A LETTER

A   Bob Dylan
B   Lay Lady Lay
C   Highway
D   Positively Fourth Street
E   Musical Youth
F   Sugar Sugar
G   Units
H   Suits
I   Uncle
J   House
K   High Noon
L   The Goons
M   Woo Woo
N   Count
O   Coon
P   Good
Q   Not
R   No One
S   Tongue
T   Gone Gone
U   Tut
V   See
W   Dee
X   A E A E
Y   Comet
Z   Neat

Quotation from 'Like a Rolling Stone', copyright Warner Brothers Music

QUIZ 60
SPACE ODDITY

1 Derrick Morgan
2 Earth Wind and Fire
3 The Milky Way
4 Halley's Comet (hence Bill Haley and the Comets)
5 The Randells in 'The Martian Hop'
6 Annabel L'win from Bow Wow Wow
7 Pink Floyd in 'Astronomy Domine' from 'Piper At The Gates Of Dawn'
8 'Saturnalia'
9 The Beatles' 'Across The Universe'
10 The Rolling Stones on 'Satanic Majesty's Request' (covered by Danse Society)

QUIZ 61
STRANGER IN PARADISE

1 Telly Savalas
2 Kids From *Fame*
3 Barry Sadler
4 Clive Dunn
5 Kenny Everett
6 Judge Dread
7 The Singing Nun
8 The Muppets
9 Jon Pertwee
10 John Cleese
11 Jane Fonda
12 Steve Wright
13 Paul Shane
14 Hot Gossip
15 Terry Wogan

1 Placido Domingo
2 Tottenham Hotspur FA Cup Final Squad
3 Sir Winston Churchill
4 Mike Harding
5 The Four Bucketeers
6 Peter Cook
7 Tony Blackburn
8 Ed Byrnes
9 Wilfred Brambell and Harry H Corbett
10 Jane Birkin and Serge Gainsbourg
11 Lorne Greene
12 Topol
13 Radha Krishna Temple
14 Allan Sherman
15 England World Cup Squad

1 Walter Brennan
2 Sister Janet Mead
3 Gerrard Hoffnung
4 Rutles
5 Keith Michell
6 The Singing Dogs
7 Tom Lehrer
8 Paul Burnett and Dave Lee Travis
9 Victor Lundberg
10 Jose Ferrer
11 Richard Dimbleby
12 Rick Dees
13 Liverpool Football Team
14 Obernkirchen Children's Choir
15 Dorothy Provine

ANSWERS

QUIZ 62
MERRY XMAS EVERYBODY

 A

1   1982
2   Brenda Lee
3   Chubby Checker and Bobby Rydell
4   A Beatle!
5   'Lonely This Christmas'
6   Elton John
7   'Smurfland'
8   Holly and the Ivys
9   The Snowmen
10 Miss Snob and Class 3c

 B

1   1967
2   Bing Crosby and the Dickies
3   'Santa Claus Is Back In Town'
4   Greg Lake
5   'Be Bop A Lula'
6   Chris Hill
7   The Ronettes
8   Dickie Valentine
9   Harlem Community Choir
10 'One Nine For Santa'

 C

1   1976
2   'Little Drummer Boy'
3   'Run Rudolph Run'
4   Eddie Cochran
5   Bob Dylan
6   Wolfman Jack
7   JUNE!! of 1956
8   Baby's
9   'And Now The Waltz (C'Est La Vie)'
10 Phil Lynott and Scott Gorham from Thin Lizzy and Paul Cook and
    Steve Jones from the Sex Pistols.

QUIZ 63
YOU KNOW MY NAME . . . LOOK UP MY NUMBER

1   Shirley Ellis
2   Sister Sledge
3   Moody Blues
4   Genesis
5   Smokey Robinson and the Miracles
6   Iron Maiden
7   Classix Nouveaux
8   Jona Lewie
9   Yardbirds
10   Sparks
11   Rolling Stones
12   Joe Brown
13   David Cassidy, or Barry Manilow
14   Eddie Cochran
15   Wings
16   Bobby Darin
17   Mamas and the Papas, or the Shirelles
18   42   59   Billy Williams or more recently Barry Manilow
19   Selector
20   Chairmen of the Board
21   Beatles
22   Nolans
23   Medicine Head
24   Vic Damone
25   Monkees
26   Clifford T Ward
27   Cliff Richard
28   Fischer Z
29   Jethro Tull
30   Herman's Hermits
31   Cookies
32   Adam Faith

33   Sandy Nelson
34   Barron Knights
35   Melanie
36   Blondie
37   Elvis Presley
38   Ray Charles, or Jerry Lee Lewis
39   Boomtown Rats
40   Beach Boys
41   Beatles
42   See 18
43   Leo Sayer
44   Shirelles
45   Manfred Mann
46   Tom Tom Club
47   Robert Palmer
48   David Essex
49   Rod Stewart, P P Arnold
50   Tom Jones
51   Squeeze
52   Scorpions
53   Men At Work
54   Dave Clark Five
55   Nolans
56   Funkadelic
57   Frankie Vaughan
58   Stealer's Wheel
59   See 18
60   David Bowie
61   Tony Bennett
62   Slade
63   Beatles

MORE QUESTIONS THAN ANSWERS

If you have cruised through the preceding quizzes without having to think too hard then this final quiz is for you. Between us we have devised 100 tricky questions. Some are based on facts that were tucked away quietly in one corner of the music press; others require a certain amount of lateral thinking to fathom the connection between groups and/or songs. Those of you who cruised through the preceding quizzes by constantly cheating and looking at the answers will now come unstuck because we haven't printed the answers to these questions.

The first reader to send us a complete list of 100 correct answers will qualify for a free copy of each subsequent edition of The Guinness Book of British Hit Singles for life.

We have 50 GRRR Level certificates signed by the authors of this book to give to the senders of the fifty best scores. You have until 31 Dec. 1984 to send your answers to:

More Questions Than Answers,

Guinness Superlatives,

2 Cecil Court,

London Road,

ENFIELD,

Middx.

After the above date you can send a stamped, self addressed envelope to the above address and we will send you a list of the answers.

Good luck to you all.

1 If Frank Sinatra and Kiki Dee toured America together what city would they be certain to play?

2 In what sense could Thomas Dolby be called Lene Lovich's toy boy?

3 Why might Sammy Davis Jr. think he owes part of his career to Napoleon?

4 Why might Lita Roza have a weakness for the song 'Oh Susanna'?

5 Why was 'Revolver' the Beatles' most civil album?

6 Who would Andy Gibb and Frankie Valli be most likely to gossip about?

7 To where would the Shadows and Donovan go on a package tour?

8 Why might the Beatles have been unhappy the week 'She Loves You' returned to number one after a 4-week absence?

9 Most acts cannot wait to earn a Greatest Hits album. Why might Roxy Music have regretted issuing theirs?

10 Why should Alfred Hitchcock have loved the Chipmunks?

11 At Elizabeth Taylor's 50th birthday party the disc jockey was told he could play any record he chose except for one, a UK number two in 1957. What was so sensitive about this single?

12 When the Clash needed a new guitarist, why could they have been expected to audition Al Caiola?

13 There is only one single of which it can truthfully be said 'We will never know how long it would have been number one.' Which record is that?

14 If the Newbeats re-formed, they could choose David Gates, Paul Weller or Paul Young as their lead singer. Why?

15 *Curtain Up* lifted the curtain up on what?

16 Radio 1 disc jockeys have occasionally charted with random hits, but which DJ was in an actual group that scored five top forty entries?

17 Elton John waited until he was in America to do something he had never done in Britain. He did it five times. What was it?

18 What Los Angeles quintet could have been Mao Tse-Tung's favourite pop group?

19 The marriage of which chart stars would give someone the name Dee Dee Dee?

20 What Andy Williams song would Frank Chacksfield be most likely to record if he made his own musical autobiography?

21 Why might Geoff Love share the bill with Dr Hook?

22 If Neil Sedaka were to make a video LP, which of his songs would be likely be made by the award-winning producer Mike Nesmith?

23 Davy Crockett was one of America's greatest frontier heroes. Yet he let Tennessee Ernie Ford down. How?

24 What song did it take Paul McCartney 95 years to cover and who recorded the original version?

25 Though they have never played jazz, Hot Chocolate might have conceivably recorded with the Modern Jazz Quartet. How?

26 What is the connection between Van McCoy and the England cricket captain of 1972–3?

27 What is the connection between Sheb Wooley and Admiral Lord Nelson?

28 Which UK Top Ten single on the London label was issued on both 45 and 78 rpm with a mastering fault that caused the music to slow down for a moment before returning to normal?

29 'The Duchess' released 'Dynamite Rag' in 1953. Under what name did she enjoy several British chart hits in later years?

30 What do these three records have in common: 'Cathy's Clown' by the Everly Brothers, 'Palisades Park' by Freddy Cannon, and 'Little Drummer Boy' by the Harry Simeone Chorale?

31 Why is there a difference of 2·6 between Rudy Martinez and James Barry Keefer?

32 Complete the following sequence: London-American, Fontana, Oriole, Stateside, —?

33 Why is Garry Mills unlikely to be a fan of Buzz Cason?

34 Which 1966 US hit written by one of the most successful songwriters of the rock era contained the line 'You read your Emily Dickinson and I my Robert Frost'?

35 And which 1982 UK hit contained a reference to feminist writer Marilyn French?

36 Which one of his many other recorded tracks would Frank Sinatra associate with 'Learnin' The Blues' and 'Five Minutes More'?

37 Which major male vocalist (20 years of more or less continuous success) wrote the following sleeve note for one of his biggest US albums?: 'I can't see anything wrong with sex between consenting anybodies. I think we make far too much of it. After all, one's genitals are just one important part of the magnificent human body.'

38 Who was the leader of Tico and The Triumphs?

39 What is the connection between Long John Baldry and Bob Beamon?

40 Which major recording act's first UK single release was (a) 'Don't Rain On My Parade' (b) 'The Wizard' (c) 'I've Been Loving You'?

41 Which group had both Chas Hodges and Ritchie Blackmore simultaneously in its line-up?

42 What do Reg Ball and Declan McManus have in common?

43 Fill in the gap: The Beatles, Mary Hopkin, —, The Black Dyke Mills Band.

44 Why would Mike McGear have been a little disappointed by the success of Peter Sarstedt's 'Where Do You Go To My Lovely'?

45 What career move was common to Keith Richards, Dionne Warwick and Smokie?

46 Which US chart-topping album contains the tracks 'Spaced Cowboy', 'Thank You For Talkin' To Me Africa' and 'Luv N' Haight'?

47 What has John Le Carre's sister got in common with David Harman?

48 What links the Marathons, the Cadets, the Jayhawks and the Vibrations?

49 Who were John Gummoe, Eddie Snyder, Dave Wilson, Dave Stevens and Dave Zabo?

50 Who starred in two films which provided number one hit singles, but never had a hit single himself?

51 A famous American artist recorded a Bacharach–David theme for yet another film starring the actor in the previous question, but it was too late to be included in the movie. Name the singer and the song?

52 Which number one hit single recording artist also played county cricket for Essex?

53 What has Mrs Annie Bannister of Liverpool got to do with 'Rock Around The Clock'?

54 What is the connection between Elmo Glick and Muhammad Ali?

55 What have 'Wooden Heart', 'Billy Don't Be A Hero' and 'You Can't Hurry Love' in common?

56 What have 'Mandy' by Barry Manilow and 'Nine To Five' by Sheena Easton in common?

57 Which number one hitmaker was born in Woodside Street, Cindertord, Gloucestershire?

58 Which number one hit songwriter ran for President of the United States in 1952?

59 In 1970, a best-selling LP featured a track called 'We Are Not Helpless'. Among the musicians helping out on this track were Ringo Starr, Rita Coolidge, John Sebastian, Booker T Jones and Cass Elliott. Who was the vocalist?

60 Who played lead guitar on Phil Lynott's tribute to Elvis Presley, 'King's Call'?

61 Who was the Glaswegian who joined Ken Colyer's Jazzmen in 1952, Chris Barber's Jazzband in 1954, and formed his own band in 1956?

62 What was the title of the first Shadows' single after 'Apache' not to make the British charts?

63 Who changed their name from Billy Lee and the Rivierras after a suggestion by Bob Crewe and then went on to have American chart success?

64 From which band did Dave Rowberry come when he replaced Alan Price on keyboards in the Animals?

65 Which band performed 'Remember You' in a Laurence Olivier film, and what was the film?

66 What comes next in this sequence? 'The Story Of My Life', 'Magic Moments', 'Anyone Who Had A Heart', 'Always Something There to Remind Me', ...

67 A song written in 1898 and originally sung by 'coon delineator' Eugene Stratton at the Oxford Music Hall reached number one in England less than 60 years later. What was the song, who wrote it and who took it to number one?

68 Who performed on all of the following albums? 'Ghost Of Princes In Towers', 'Rage In Eden', 'The Anvil'.

69 What is the next record in this sequence? 'Do You Love Me?' by Brian Poole and the Tremeloes, 'Silence Is Golden' by the Tremeloes, 'Ballad Of Bonnie and Clyde' by Georgie Fame, ...

70 What have Jimmy Young's 'Unchained Melody' and Slade's 'Merry Xmas Everybody' in common, apart from the fact that they were both number one hits?

71 What is the most widely used surname in British chart history?

72 Which chart-topping act has recorded all these songs: 'Are You Lonesome Tonight?', 'Bad Bad Leroy Brown', 'Bang Bang', 'Isn't She Lovely?', 'Just The Way You Are', 'Mrs Robinson', 'My Way' and 'Winchester Cathedral'?

73 Between her successes with 'It's A Heartache' and 'Total Eclipse Of The Heart', Bonnie Tyler won a major international song contest, defeating artists such as Paul Nicholas, Cissy Houston and Peter Noone. What was the contest, where was it held and what was Miss Tyler's winning song?

74 Cliff Richard's first hit 'Move It' was originally the B-side of the single. What was the original A-side, and who had the American hit version of the song?

75 Which number one recording artists

a) released an LP in 1983 called 'Love Songs For Night People'?

b) recorded a version of 'Tell Laura I Love Her' in 1960 which was never a hit?

c) began his recording career with 'Four Leaf Clover Blues/Too Many Parties, Too Many Pals'?

76 Who played guitar on Ike and Tina Turner's 'Nutbush City Limits'?

77 What occurred at 4.00 am on 2 July 1953?

78 In one of their Christmas shows the Beatles performed their own version of *A Midsummer Night's Dream*. Which parts did they play?

79 Who compèred Buddy Holly and the Crickets British tour over 10 years before having a number one hit of his own?

80 What is the connection between the following songs: 'All The Young Dudes' – Mott The Hoople, 'Kool In The Kaftan' – B. A. Robertson, 'Do You Remember Rock 'n' Roll Radio?' – The Ramones and 'You Better You Bet' – The Who?

81 Who has had the longest gap between British chart hits?

82 Why might McLemore Avenue be described as a quieter street than Abbey Road?

83 What connects the following songs: 'If' – Telly Savalas, 'So You Win Again' – Hot Chocolate, 'Lip Up Fatty' – Bad Manners and 'Is It A Dream?' – Classix Nouveaux?

84 He sang gospel music, American beer commercials and prominent support vocals on a Sam Cooke classic. Who is he and what was the Sam Cooke song?

85 What is the link between Duran Duran's 'Hungry Like The Wolf', Elton John's 'I'm Still Standing' and Billy Joel's 'Pressure'?

86 What distinction is shared by Thunderclap Newman and Otway and Barrett?

87 The Beatles' 'Please Please Me' was originally written in the style of which artist?

88 What is the connection between Lene Lovich, Paul Anka and Rod McKuen?

89 Who released their 'Greatest Hits' album in Britain seven years before they first made the British singles charts?

90 Who had a Japanese number one with a song singing the praises of a Scottish teeny-bop band?

91 What is the connection between Keith West, Olivia Newton-John and the musical Annie?

92 What is special about Thursday?

93 What do Andy Williams and Karen Young have in common?

94 What is the chart connection between Elvis Presley and Laurel and Hardy?

95 What political event made Roy Orbison the first of a kind?

96 What chart record did Harry Belafonte set on 10 January 1958, which remains unequalled in 1984?

97 If Abba begat ABBA, which group could be renamed BEGAT?

98 What film links 'Goodbye Mr Chips' and 'Idle On Parade' via four number one hits?

99 Which chart-topping star was once a regular on WFIL's 'Teen Time' under the name Sonny Edwards?

100 Why might Duran Duran be expected to record a version of the Buggles 'Clean Clean'?